The Great Canadian Cookbook

A Celebration of Great Canadian Cooking

Bunny Barss

The Great Canadian Cookbook
By Bunny Barss

Copyright© 1987, 2004 by Deadwood Publishing Limited

Canadian Cataloguing in Publication Data
  Barss, Beulah M., 1931-
  Oh, Canada!
  Includes index.

1. Cookery, Canadian.
2. Food habits – Canada– History. I. Title

TX715.B37 1987   641.5971   C87-098063-7

Original line drawings by Sheila Miller.

Printed in China

Mud Puddle Books, Inc.
54 West 21st Street
Suite 601
New York, New York 10010
info@mudpuddlebooks.com

ISBN 1-594120-19-6

Metric Conversion

Recipes in The Great Canadian Cookbook are given in both standard and metric measurements. All have been tested in the standard measurements but have not been tested specifically with the metric conversions.

The standard measurements have been converted to metric by a method known as common metric replacement, a method that does not produce exact equivalents but comes close. Exact conversions sometimes result in awkward fractions and sizes, so the replacement method round up or down for ease in measuring.

Table of Contents

Acknowledgments
● ● ● ● ● ● ● ● ● ● ●

This book has come to life with the help of many people. Norma Bannerman, B.Sc., dietitian, food consultant and a certified member of the International Association of Cooking Professionals, provided valuable assistance with recipe selection, testing and editing.

History and recipes came from many sources, museums, archives, diaries, letters, history books and recipe books from Newfoundland to British Columbia. Maurice Tanguay, St. Lambert, Québec made available "Recettes de Cuisine de la famille Maurice Tanguay". Glenna Gaunce, St. John, New Brunswick gave valuable advice about life in New Brunswick. Dorothy Lomas provided us with Yukon recipes belonging to the Scott family. Recipes and ideas also came from Penny Williams in Vancouver, Joan Ross in Calgary and many, many others.

Thanks to my family and friends for their enthusiastic sampling of Canadian Celebration Foods and finally many thanks to Nancy Millar for her creativity as editor and publisher.

About the Author
● ● ● ● ● ● ● ● ● ● ●

Beulah (Bunny) Barss graduated in Home Economics from the University of Saskatchewan, completed a Dietetic Internship at the Royal Victoria Hospital in Montreal and an M.A. from the University of Calgary.

She has combined her interests in history and food in the "Pioneer Cook", a historical view of prairie food, and in "Come'n Get It", a collection of ranching and pioneer stories and recipes. She has also authored two souvenir cookbooks.

Why We Eat What We Eat

I want to tell you about Canadian cooking – what it is and how it came to be – and to leave on record a collection of well-tasted Canadian recipes that can be mixed and matched for proud presentation at Canadian celebrations and festive occasions.

Preparing this book has taken a lifetime of good Canadian food experiences from childhood days in Saskatchewan – watching my mother prepare for the harvesters, eating fresh chicken fried golden brown, picking Saskatoon berries on the banks of the Wood River, roasting wieners at Buffalo Lake near Moose Jaw.

I lived (mostly ate) for one glorious year in Montreal – Sugar Pie, frogs' legs, oysters, French cooking… heady things for a prairie girl!

Later, I camped at Long Beach on Vancouver Island with my husband and children and we cooked salmon, fresh from a fishing boat, over a beach fire of driftwood. We hiked the West Coast Trail and feasted on fresh crab along the way, boiled in an old saucepan over a one-burner camp stove.

On the other side of the country, we jigged for cod off Prince Edward Island and fought fiercely over which of the incredibly delicious lobster suppers we would attend. The Cod and Scrunchions served in the Newfoundland Hotel, the Chowders of Nova Scotia, the Atlantic Salmon in Fredericton – these are food memories worth keeping.

Have you ever driven through the Ontario countryside at Thanksgiving? There are baskets of apples everywhere. An Ottawa friend served Baked Apples with Mincemeat and it is my favorite dessert to this day.

I have a special love for Manitoba. From the banks of its Red River which still carry ghosts of the voyageurs with their bright sashes to the Mennonite village. Where I stuffed myself on fresh breads, biscuits and jam in the village bakehouse as we watched bread cook in the outdoor bake oven.

Another cherished food experience was Roast Beef served from a chuckwagon during June branding at the lovely OH Ranch in the Alberta foothills. Pumpkin pies at Thanksgiving, fruit cake from a knapsack high in the Rockies, a July 1st picnic at the Millarville Races near Calgary. All these form part of my own personal Canadian food celebration.

Another very special Canadian meal, for me, was presented by chef John Walker and his staff at the Calgary Chamber of Commerce during Native Awareness Week. After considerable research, they presented a feast of native foods.

Two soups began the feast – Salmon Roe Soup with Saskatoon Berries and Corn and Squash Chowder. Fresh Bannock accompanied each soup.

After the soup course, we served ourselves from a long buffet table decorated with grains, grasses, cranberries and Smoked Salmon spread over willow sticks. What a choice – Roasted Buffalo, Broiled Rabbit with Rice Au Gratin, Smoked Salmon, Rainbow Trout, Steamed Mussels and Clams, Fiddlehead Greens. Some recipes were not quite authentic – there was no eulachon oil to dip the salmon in, no bear grease for frying the trout – but it was a wonderful day and a wonderful display of the native food tradition.

There was barely room for dessert but I nevertheless had to try baked Indian Cornmeal Pudding, Wild Berry Cobbler, Steamed Cranberry Pudding, Pumpkin and Saskatoon Pie. Delicious and interesting!

In this book, I have tried to include the best distinctively Canadian recipes, and I explain how they came to be part of our heritage. The recipes are not fancy. They are the honest food that we've enjoyed for years, updated to modern methods. Above all, they are wonderfully delicious because they taste like home. They are home!

The Story of Canadian Cooking

The story of Canadian cooking begins with the native people who lived here for centuries before the fur traders and explorers from Europe arrived. Their experiences deserve a book to themselves, for their story is one of wondrous adaptation to the circumstances around them. Depending on the region, some tribes had a plentiful supply of food; others merely eked out an existence.

Their staples were foods they found around them – salmon, cod, whitefish, caribou, moose, buffalo, rabbit and other types of game and fish; wild rice, wild berries such as blueberries and cranberries, maple syrup and birch syrup, wild plants, roots, bark and fungi. Corn, beans and pumpkin (squash included) were grown in parts of eastern Canada.

It was the native people who performed the first food processing in Canada. West coast tribes collected tons of tiny fish, eulachon, boiled them and saved the prize oil for storage in the bladders of fish and sea mammals. Prairie tribes dried meat and mixed it with fat and berries for pemmican. Bones were boiled for marrow and sausages made from animal intestines.

Many of these foods became so familiar that we forgot their origin. Some have become "gourmet" foods – such as salmon, wild rice and maple products. For many natives, foods such as caribou and moose are still important for existence, while in other areas caribou and moose would only be found in specialty restaurants.

Foods of the Indians and methods of cooking and preserving saved many of the fur traders, explorers and early settlers from starvation. Pemmican fed the work force of the fur trade on the prairies as did salmon on the west coast. Corn, beans and pumpkin fed settlers in eastern Canada – sometimes three times a day! Recipes brought from the old country had to be modified in this new world so, for instance, dried saskatoons and blueberries sometimes went into Christmas puddings in place of raisins, buffalo tallow was used in place of beef suet.

Gradually, Canada became settled by people from all over the world. Again and again, old ways were adapted and evolved into a new distinctive cuisine. A Canadian cuisine. For instance, women from France learned to make their traditional "tartes" with blueberries.

English housewives gathered fiddlehead greens in the New Brunswick forests; they weren't the Brussels sprouts of home, but they were fresh, green and tasty.

And so on it went... old ways meeting new realities, resulting in a distinctive blend. A distinctive taste. The Canadian taste.

Some say our cooking is regional, although in most cases the so-called regional food is enjoyed across the country. Thus, we may associate lobster with Prince Edward Island and beef with Alberta but indeed, both are served and enjoyed across the country. Nova Scotia is often credited with blueberries but again – you can find blueberries in every part of the country. Indeed, there are two blueberry festivals held every year in opposite corners of this vast land – one in Lac St. Jean, Québec and one in Fort McMurray, Alberta.

Consider the humble cranberry. They're enjoyed in the far north by the Inuit, they were a favorite in earlier days in northern fur forts, they're a tradition in the maritimes and just recently, I sampled cranberry sauce made from wild cranberries picked on a prairie ranch. They too have a way of turning up all over Canada. The jelly roll is another example. On the prairies, it's served up as a quick fresh roll cake. But in Québec, it's given considerably more ceremony – decorated to resemble a Yule log and served, especially on Christmas Eve, as the Bûche de Noël. In spite of their regional differences, these two cakes are sisters under the skin.

In most Canadian kitchens, a ham bone is automatically saved for French Canadian Pea Soup, and in restaurants, coffee is best accompanied by a muffin... no matter where you live. We're not all alike across this vast country of ours... but we're not as different as we might think, either. Which is why I've collected, tested and enjoyed the distinctive Canadian recipes that follow in this book.

I believe passionately that we have Canadian food traditions, that there is a distinctive Canadian taste. That taste is good, delicious, worthy of knowing and repeating.

Come celebrate Canadain food with me!

Canada Day Family Picnic

On July 1, we celebrate our land – huge, gentle and beautiful... for on this day in 1867 representatives from four regions gathered in Charlottetown, Prince Edward Island, and voted to unite with "One Dominion under the name of Canada".

Canada has grown since then to stretch from the Atlantic Ocean to the Pacific Ocean to the Arctic Ocean. We have grown in spirit, mind and heart, and made a home for people of every ethnic background who choose to live in freedom. This is what we celebrate.

And celebrate we do, with concerts and dancing on Parliament Hill in Ottawa, to parades and pancake breakfasts in Newfoundland, to a lamb barbecue on Saturna Island, British Columbia. There are Folk Festivals in Manitoba and Fisherman's Regattas in Nova Scotia. There are rodeos, horse races, raft races, soapbox derbies, dances, festivals and carnivals. In Yellowknife, the midnight sun finds children playing in the streets until 1:00 a.m. We invite you to celebrate Canada Day along with us... with a picnic in the great outdoors.

MENU
● ● ● ●

Orangeade
Oven-Fried Parmesan Chicken
Picnic Potato Salad
Green Bean Salad
Quick Whole Wheat Loaf
Watermelon Chunks
Oatmeal Cookies... page 49
Chocolate Cake with Rocky Mountain Icing OR
White Layer Cake with Coconut Celebration Icing OR
Lost Lemon Cake... page 210
Homemade Ice Cream
Roasting Marshmallows

Orangeade

This delicious orange concentrate can be stored in the refrigerator and used as needed. Or make up a batch and take it along to the picnic, adding cold water on the spot.

4	4	oranges
3	3	lemons
4 tablespoons	60 mL (60 g)	citric acid*
6 cups	1.5 L	boiling water
6 cups	1.5 L	sugar
		cold water and ice cubes as required

Chop whole oranges and lemons in blender or food processor until fine. Dissolve citric acid in boiling water. Add sugar and fruit mixture. Let stand overnight. Strain and store. Use 3 parts cold water to 1 part orange concentrate.

Yields 50 to 60 servings or 10 quarts (10 L).

Note: You can buy citric acid at any drug store.

Oven-Fried Parmesan Chicken

This crunchy chicken – served hot or cold – is easy and delicious. Make your own breadcrumbs or buy them packaged. Use a whole fryer or chicken breasts.

1 cup	250 mL	dry breadcrumbs
½ cup	125 mL	Parmesan cheese
¼ teaspoon	1 mL	garlic powder
Dash	Dash	freshly ground pepper
4	4	chicken breasts
⅓ cup	75 mL	melted butter

Preheat oven to 325°F (160°C). Mix crumbs, cheese, garlic powder and pepper. Dip each piece of chicken in melted butter and roll in crumbs. Place chicken, skin side up, in lightly greased baking dish. Don't let pieces touch.

Bake uncovered for about one hour. Refrigerate if serving cold. Otherwise, dish it up and enjoy the compliments!

Serves 4 to 5.

Picnic Potato Salad

This delicious and slightly different potato salad is a good choice for picnics since it has vinaigrette dressing and goes well with cold meats and fresh vegetables.

4 cups	1 L	diced potatoes
		(new potatoes are best)
⅓ cup	75 mL	vegetable oil
2 tablespoons	30 mL	vinegar
½ teaspoon	2 mL	salt
¼ teaspoon	1 mL	pepper
½ cup	125 mL	chopped green onions

Scrub potatoes with brush and boil in salted water until tender but still firm. Cool and dice. In jar, shake oil, vinegar, salt and pepper and combine with potatoes. Sprinkle chopped green onions over top. Mix lightly and chill. Carry in cooler to picnic.

Serves 4 to 5.

Green Bean Salad

This dish is delicious served as a salad or vegetable, and can be made with frozen or fresh green or yellow beans. Make it early in the day and refrigerate for later.

4 cups	1 L	green beans
1	1	medium onion, thinly sliced
½ teaspoon	2 mL	sugar
½ teaspoon	2 mL	salt
¾ cup	175 mL	sour cream
1 tablespoon	15 mL	vinegar
1 tablespoon	15 mL	sugar
		salt and freshly ground pepper to taste

Wash and schnipple beans – in other words, cut them diagonally in very thin slices. Or leave them whole.

Boil in salted water until just tender. Drain and cool.

Slice onion very thin, sprinkle with ½ teaspoon (2 mL) each of sugar and salt and cover with water. Allow to stand 10 minutes. Drain thoroughly.

Mix sour cream, vinegar, sugar, salt and pepper and combine with cooled beans and drained onions. Chill.

Serves 4 to 5.

Quick Whole-Wheat Loaf

To serve this moist and tasty bread at a picnic, take along a bread board so that guests can cut their own slices. Again and again!

2 cups	500 mL	whole-wheat flour
2 cups	500 mL	all-purpose flour
2 tablespoons	30mL	brown sugar
2 teaspoons	10 mL	baking powder
1 teaspoon	5 mL	baking soda
1 teaspoon	5 mL	salt
¼ cup	50 mL	melted butter
1	1	egg, beaten
2 cups	500 mL	buttermilk
		oatmeal flakes
		OR granola to coat loaf

Preheat oven to 375°F (190°C).

Combine all dry ingredients. Mix butter, egg and buttermilk and stir into dry ingredients. Sprinkle oatmeal flakes or granola on counter.

Place dough on flakes, knead for one minute and shape in round loaf. The outside of loaf should be covered with oatmeal or granola.

Cut across top and place on greased baking pan. Bake 45 to 50 minutes or until nicely browned.

Yields 1 loaf.

Homemade Ice Cream

Homemade ice cream evokes all sorts of memories – hot summer afternoons -- kids fighting over who gets the first lick. Sparkling ice cream in the best dessert dishes. Add fresh berries in season.

1 cup	250 mL	sugar
¼ teaspoon	1 mL	salt
2 cups	500 mL	milk
3	3	eggs, beaten
2 cups	500 mL	whipping cream
2 teaspoons	10 mL	vanilla

In deep bowl, beat sugar, salt, milk and eggs well.

Stir in whipping cream and vanilla, then pour in ice cream container.

Pack outside tub with layers of salt and ice.

Turn freezer handle at slow steady pace until turning becomes very difficult – approximately 20 to 30 minutes. Follow the manufacturer's directions if using an electric freezer.

Remove gear case. Wipe off cover, remove the dasher.

The ice cream can be eaten immediately or the tub can be packed with ice and salt, covered with a blanket and left for an hour or two to harden.

Yields 3 quarts (3 L).

Chocolate Cake with Rocky Mountain Icing

*This moist cake – baked in a square cake pan – is perfect for a picnic...
delicious and easy to carry. If you want a bigger cake, a layered cake,
just double the recipe.*

1½ cups	375 mL	flour
1 cup	250 mL	sugar
4 tablespoons	60 mL	cocoa
1 teaspoon	5 mL	baking powder
½ teaspoon	2 mL	baking soda
¼ teaspoon	1 mL	salt
½ cup	125 mL	melted margarine
1 cup	250 mL	lukewarm water
1 teaspoon	5 mL	vinegar
1 teaspoon	5 mL	vanilla

Preheat oven to 350°F (180°C).

Sift flour, sugar, cocoa, baking powder, baking soda and salt.

Mix margarine, water, vinegar and vanilla. Add to dry ingredients
and beat until well mixed.

Bake 30 minutes in greased 8" or 9" square pan (1.5 L) or 9" round
pan.

If doubling the recipe, bake in 2 round pans or in one 9" x 13" (4
L) cake pan. The cake in the larger pan will require about 30 to 45
minutes.

Rocky Mountain Icing

This icing – so named because the marshmallows peek through the chocolate frosting like so many snow-topped mountains – is slightly unusual but a wonderful finish for any cake. Enough for 8" (1.5 L) square cake.

1½ cups	375 mL	miniature marshmallows
¼ cup	50 mL	butter OR margarine
¼ cup	50 mL	cocoa
1 cup	250 mL	icing (confectioner's) sugar
		boiling water,
		enough to thin icing

Sprinkle marshmallows over surface of cake immediately after removing from oven.

Combine butter or margarine, cocoa and icing sugar.

Add just enough boiling water to make icing slightly thinner than the usual butter icing.

Drizzle over surface of marshmallows, filling in all nooks and crannies.

White Layer Cake with Coconut Celebration Icing

This easy-to-make cake makes two, 9" (23 cm) layers or three, 8" (20 cm) layers. Covered with fluffy icing and sprinkled with coconut, it's a perfect birthday cake. Perfect for any celebration, for that matter!

⅔ cup	150 mL	shortening
1⅔ cups	400 mL	berry sugar
1 teaspoon	5 mL	vanilla
4	4	egg whites
3 cups	750 mL	cake flour
3 teaspoons	15 mL	baking powder
1 teaspoon	5 mL	salt
1½ cups	375 mL	milk

Preheat oven to 375° (190°C).

Cream shortening, sugar and vanilla until light and fluffy. Add unbeaten egg whites, one at a time beating well after each addition.

Sift cake flour before measuring. Sift again with baking powder and salt.

Fold flour mixture and milk alternately in first mixture. Pour in greased layer-cake pans.

Bake 25 to 30 minutes until a toothpick inserted into the center of the cake comes out clean.

Cool in pans for 5 minutes, then loosen from sides and invert on rack.

When thoroughly cool, assemble with filling and icing as follows.

(Continued on next page.)

(Continued)

Coconut Celebration Icing

		apricot OR peach jam
1½ cups	375 mL	whipping cream
3 tablespoons	45 mL	sugar
2 teaspoons	10 mL	vanilla
1 cup	250 mL	grated coconut

Put cake layers together with apricot or peach jam.

Whip cream until stiff, fold in sugar and vanilla. Cover top and sides of cake.

Spread coconut in flat pan, toast under broiler until golden. Sprinkle over cake.

Note: If you don't have cake flour, use regular white flour. Just cut the amount by about ⅓ cup (75 mL).

Notes

Canada Day Elegant Picnic

CANADA DAY has traditionally been celebrated with picnics across the country, but picnics don't have to mean humble fare. If you want the best of three worlds, serve an elegant picnic in the great Canadian outdoors in honor of a great Canadian occasion!

MENU
● ● ● ●

Chilled Filet of Beef
Dijon Mustard
Lobster Tails with Lemon Mayonnaise
Powerful Pasta Salad
Sliced Tomatoes with Basil... page 117
Dill Pickles
French Bread, Unsalted Butter
Fresh Whole Strawberries
Lemon Coconut Squares OR
Triple Chocolate Slice

Other Occasions For A Picnic In Canada

At the Millarville Races
On Cavendish Beach
Before the Play at Stratford
In a Rocky Mountain Meadow
Boating Excursions in the Bay
An Outdoor Concert
After the Rodeo

Chilled Filet of Beef

A filet of beef cooked medium rare and served cold is an impressive way to begin an elegant picnic or any other special meal!

3 pounds	1.5 kg	filet of beef
1	1	garlic clove, slivered
		salt and freshly ground pepper

Preheat oven to 450°F (230°C).

Make tiny slits in beef and insert slivers of garlic. Salt and pepper this meat and place in shallow roasting pan.

Bake meat for 30 minutes or until meat thermometer registers 140°F (60°C), or "rare".

Chill and slice very thin. Reassemble, wrap in plastic wrap and carry to picnic in cooler.

Serves 8.

Lobster Tails

Use fresh or frozen lobster tails. If frozen, thaw to room temperature. Drop either fresh or thawed into boiling water and simmer for about 8 minutes.

Chill and keep chilled.

Make Lemon Mayonnaise by adding a generous squeeze of fresh lemon juice to the mayonnaise.

Powerful Pasta Salad

This gently spiced salad combines powerfully with cold meat and sliced tomatoes – just what our Canada Day picnic calls for!

2 cups	500 mL	uncooked shell pasta
⅓ cup	75 mL	sour cream
⅓ cup	75 mL	mayonnaise
½ teaspoon	2 mL	curry powder
½ teaspoon	2 mL	salt
¼ teaspoon	1 mL	freshly ground pepper
¼ cup	50 mL	chopped green onions
¼ cup	50 mL	chopped fresh parsley
½ cup	125 mL	small green peas
½ cup	125 mL	thinly sliced celery
1 cup	250 mL	grated cheddar cheese

Cook pasta until just tender in boiling salted water. Drain.

Combine sour cream, mayonnaise, curry powder, salt, pepper, green onions and parsley. Mix with the drained pasta.

Cook peas briefly – just to tender crisp stage. Add with celery and cheese to pasta mixture. Mix lightly. Adjust seasonings. Keep chilled until serving time.

Serves 8.

Lemon Coconut Squares

Luscious mouth-watering Lemon Squares are best made the day before serving. They store and freeze well, and finish up a summer picnic with panache!

Base and Topping:

10	10	soda crackers
1 cup	250 mL	flour
1 teaspoon	5 mL	baking powder
½ cup	125 mL	sugar
½ cup	125 mL	butter
1½ cups	375 mL	fine unsweetened coconut

Lemon Filling:

1 cup	250 mL	sugar
2 tablespoons	30 mL	flour
½ teaspoon	2 mL	salt
1	1	egg, beaten
1	1	lemon, juice and rind
1 cup	250 mL	boiling water
1 tablespoon	15 mL	butter

(Continued on next page.)

(Continued)

Preheat oven to 350°F (180°C).

Roll soda crackers until fine. Combine with flour, baking powder and sugar. Rub in butter to form crumbs. Add coconut. Set aside.

To make Lemon Filling, mix sugar, flour and salt ingredients together in small heavy saucepan or double boiler.

Mix egg with lemon juice and grated rind, stir into dry ingredients. Slowly stir in boiling water. Cook until thick, stirring all the while. Remove from heat and add butter. Cool slightly.

To put layers together, spread half of crumb mixture on bottom of 9" (23 cm) square cake pan. Pat down firmly.

Cover with Lemon Filling. Spread remaining crumbs on top and smooth out. Bake for 30 minutes or until crumbs are lightly browned on top.

Triple Chocolate Slice

Every now and then, you need a dynamite dessert, something that makes everyone sit back and say "Wow". Well, this is it – a wonderful new square that builds on the tradition of squares like the Nanaimo bar but goes much further!

The second layer is flavored with vanilla but could be flavored with Irish cream or apricot liqueur.

First Layer:

½ cup	125 mL	butter OR margarine
1 cup	250 mL	brown sugar
4 tablespoons	60 mL	cocoa
2	2	eggs, beaten
1 teaspoon	5 mL	vanilla
¼ teaspoon	1 mL	salt
⅔ cup	150 mL	flour

Preheat oven to 350°F (180°).

Melt butter or margarine. Combine with sugar and cocoa. Beat in eggs, vanilla (or liqueurs) and salt. Stir in flour.

Spread in a buttered 8" (20 cm) square pan. Bake for about 25 minutes or until a toothpick comes out clean. Cool. Then spread with second layer.

(Continued on next page.)

(Continued)

Second Layer:

1 tablespoon	15 mL	cocoa
4 tablespoons	60 mL	butter OR margarine
2 cups	500 mL	icing (confectioner's) sugar
3 tablespoons	45 mL	hot water
1 teaspoon	5 mL	vanilla

Beat all the ingredients together until light and fluffy.

Spread over cooled first layer and immediately place in refrigerator to chill. Then spread with third layer.

Third Layer:

2 tablespoons	30 mL	butter OR margarine
3 tablespoons	45 mL	cocoa
¾ cup	175 mL	icing (confectioner's) sugar
1½ tablespoon	22 mL	boiling water
1 teaspoon	5 mL	vanilla

Mix together. If sugar doesn't dissolve, heat the glaze. Spread over chilled second layer.

To serve, slice into long, fairly thin slices.

Notes

Thanksgiving Dinner

Thanksgiving day, "a day of General Thanksgiving to Almighty God for the bountiful harvest with which Canada has been blessed", dates right back to the time of the Loyalists. However, it wasn't until 1879 that it was proclaimed a national holiday to be celebrated November 6 every year. Then in 1957, Canada's parliament decreed that it should be observed on the second Monday of October.

The pioneers celebrated Thanksgiving with venison, duck, wild turkey, goose, seafood, cornbread, vegetables and desserts made from wild fruits. Today we celebrate with Roast Turkey or Chicken. Cranberry Sauce, vegetables, salads and Pumpkin Pie. Especially Pumpkin Pie!

MENU
● ● ● ●
Traditional Roast Turkey... page 62
Cornbread Stuffing
Cranberry Sauce... page 85
Mashed Potato Casserole
Succotash
Broccoli Spears
Pumpkin Pie with Sweetened Whipped Cream OR
Maple Mousse... page 102

Cornbread Stuffing

This beautifully seasoned stuffing is worth the extra work of preparing Cornbread. Prepare the stuffing the day before you plan to roast the turkey. The directions for roast turkey are on page 62.

1 cup	250 mL	butter OR margarine
1 cup	250 mL	chopped onions
6 cups	1.5 L	crumbled Cornbread*
6 cups	1.5 L	soft bread crumbs
½ cup	125 mL	chopped fresh parsley
1 teaspoon	5 mL	salt, sage, thyme EACH

Melt butter and sauté onions until soft. In large bowl, combine cornbread, bread crumbs, parsley and seasonings.

Add onion and butter and toss to combine well. Stuff loosely in body and neck cavities.

If there is extra stuffing, wrap in foil or place in covered casserole and bake in oven for last hour or so of roasting. If desired, drizzle a little of the turkey drippings over dressing and toss lightly to combine.

Yields 12 cups (3 L) dressing, enough for 12-14 lb. (5-6 kg) turkey.

*Note: The recipe for cornbread is on page 118. Half of the recipe baked in an 8" x 8" (22 x 20 cm) pan yields about 8 cups (2 L) of crumbs. If cornbread is baked fresh for the dressing, it can produce a very moist dressing, so be sure to pack it loosely into turkey cavities to allow for expansion.

Succotash

The combination of bright yellow corn and fresh green beans has always been a classic favorite – not just for its wonderful taste but also for its wonderful color!

4 cups	1 L	cut green beans
¾ cup	175 mL	sliced celery
4 tablespoons	60 ML	chopped onion
2 tablespoons	30 mL	butter OR margarine
1 tablespoon	15 mL	flour
⅔ cup	150 mL	milk
2 x 14 ounces	2 x 398 mL	cans niblet corn

Cook green beans until just tender. Sauté celery and onion in butter or margarine until tender.

Stir in flour, add milk and cook over low heat, stirring constantly until thickened. Drain corn and beans. Add to the milk mixture.

Heat through and serve, or refrigerate and reheat at serving time. May be necessary to add 2 to 3 teaspoons (10-15 mL) milk or water when reheating.

Serves 8 to 10.

Mashed Potato Casserole

Prepare this delicious potato casserole the day before it's to be served, and then reheat in the oven or microwave.

3 pounds	1.5 kg	potatoes (about 9)
2	2	eggs, separated
4 tablespoons	60 mL	butter
¾ – 1 cup	175-250 mL	milk
1 teaspoon	5 mL	salt
		pepper to taste
¼ teaspoon	1 mL	cream of tartar
		paprika and/or
		parmesan cheese

Boil potatoes until tender. Preheat oven to 350°F (180°C). Drain and mash.

Beat egg yolks slightly and add to potatoes along with butter, milk, salt and pepper. Beat well. Potatoes should be smooth and light but not runny. Add more milk if necessary.

Beat egg whites with cream of tartar until stiff but not dry. Fold whites into potato mixture. Spoon into greased serving casserole. Sprinkle top with paprika and/or Parmesan cheese.

At this point, you can either finish baking casserole, or you can refrigerate until needed.

Bake for about an hour, or put into microwave for about 10 minutes.

Serves 8 to 10.

Broccoli Spears

Surely there is not a more attractive and delicious vegetable than broccoli – rich green in color and tender-crisp in texture.

First, trim the spears so that they are the same length and thickness (Save the tough, lower stems for soup). Place the spears in a deep saucepan.

Add water to cover bottom (about ½" (1 cm) deep, and a dash of salt.

Cover saucepan. Bring water to a boil, then reduce heat to simmer.

Allow broccoli to steam only to the tender-crisp stage (about 8 to 10 minutes).

Serve unadorned or drizzle with melted butter and lemon juice and/or garnish with coarsely chopped toasted almonds.

Pumpkin Pie

Native Indians of eastern Canada and the United States introduced pumpkin and squash to European settlers who in turn learned to use them for everything from pancakes to jam to pie! Pumpkin pie is a classic now, almost a must for Thanksgiving!

This is a fairly standard recipe. If you'd like to vary it a bit, add 2 tablespoons (30 mL) molasses along with the brown sugar, or drizzle buckwheat honey diluted with a bit of water over the pie surface just after it comes out of the oven. Put it back in the oven for just a moment and you'll have a delicious glaze.

1	1	unbaked pie shell
1 ½ cups	375 mL	canned OR cooked pumpkin
¾ cup	175 mL	brown sugar
½ teaspoon	2 mL	ginger
½ teaspoon	2 mL	nutmeg
½ teaspoon	2 mL	cinnamon
½ teaspoon	2 mL	salt
2	2	eggs, slightly beaten
13½ ounces	385 mL	evaporated milk (1 can)

Preheat oven to 350°F (180°C).

Prepare pastry and line a fairly large pie plate – at least 9" (23 cm). Combine pumpkin, sugar, spices and salt. Add eggs and milk. Pour into unbaked shell.

Bake for 15 minutes.

Reduce heat to 350°F (180°C) and continue baking for another 45 minutes or until pie tests done.

Serve with Sweetened Whipped Cream (on page 35).

Sweetened Whipped Cream

Whipped cream is a versatile filling and topping that can be served as is, or sweetened and flavored with vanilla, lemon, liqueurs, cinnamon or chocolate.

1 cup	250 mL	whipping cream
2 tablespoons	30 mL	sugar
1 teaspoon	5 mL	vanilla

Be sure whipping cream is well chilled.

Place cream, sugar and vanilla in mixing bowl and whip until soft peaks form.

Notes

Hunters' Wild Game Buffet Dinner

The buffalo don't roam in Canada anymore; however, there are still areas where wild game and birds flourish, and where hunters are able to practice their sport. A successful hunt can result in a wonderful wild game buffet dinner for friends.

Incidentally, if you don't hunt, you can buy some of these varieties, now that formerly wild animals and birds are being raised on game farms.

Such a dinner should include at least two varieties of specially prepared game or birds. A logical (and tasty!) accompaniment for wild meat is wild rice. Also, a fruity spicy chutney or jelly should be served – something like cranberry chutney, page 65, or Red Currant Jelly.

Cap the dinner with a traditional and mouthwatering dessert such as Pumpkin Pie With Whipped Cream, page 34-35, or Apple Crisp, page 186.

MENU
● ● ● ●

Sweet and Sour Wild Duck or Goose
Pheasant in Wine
Game Bird Pie
Spiced Moose or Buffalo... page 83
Wild Rice... page 218
Jellied Apricot and Mandarin Orange Salad
Dilled Green Beans... page 77
Mixed Green Salad with Lemon Mustard Dressing... page 173
Pumpkin Pie with Sweetened Whipped cream... page 34
Apple Crisp... page 186

Game Bird Pie

Game Bird Pie was popular with early Canadian settlers; the French Canadians, the Acadians, those of English origin, all had their own special versions. This is a new all Canadian version, tasty and different!

For this recipe, you need 4 to 5 cups (1-1.25 L) cooked game bird. Two pheasants will yield this amount; most other game birds – grouse, partridge, and prairie chicken – will yield slightly less. Place birds in a heavy saucepan or Dutch oven. Fill pot half full of water. Add one tablespoon (15 mL) dried parsley. Simmer gently for 2-2 ½ hours or until meat comes away from bones easily. Remove meat in strips from bones and set aside. Save stock.

4-5 cups	1-1.25 L	cooked game bird
6 tablespoons	90 mL	butter OR margarine
1	1	large onion, chopped
2 cups	500 mL	sliced mushrooms
6 tablespoons	90 mL	flour
2 cups	500 mL	reserved stock
1 ½ cups	375 mL	light cream
½ cup	125 mL	white wine
2 teaspoons	10 mL	Worcestershire sauce
1 teaspoon	5 mL	salt
¾ teaspoon	3 mL	sage
½ teaspoon	2 mL	thyme
¼ teaspoon	1 mL	pepper
		pastry for single crust pie, page 165

Preheat oven to 350°F. (180°C)

Place cooked meat in 3-quart (3 L) deep casserole dish.

Melt butter in saucepan and sauté onion until tender. Add mushrooms and sauté lightly.

(Continued on next page.)

(Continued)

Stir in flour, then slowly add reserved stock and light cream. Simmer and stir until thickened.

Add wine and seasonings and stir to combine well. Pour sauce over game in dish.

Roll out pastry and place over top. Make 3 to 4 slits in pastry for steam to escape.

For a shiny appearance, combine 1 slightly beaten egg white with 1 tablespoon (15 mL) water and brush over surface of pastry.

Bake for 1 hour or until lightly browned and bubbling inside. Can be made ahead and frozen.

Serves 6 to 8.

Sweet and Sour Wild Goose or Duck

A wonderful way to use the ducks and geese brought home by the mighty hunters in the Fall! Use only the breasts of the birds.

3-4	3-4	whole goose OR duck breasts
2	2	eggs, slightly beaten
2 tablespoons	30 mL	water
1 cup	250 mL	fine dry bread crumbs
1 tablespoon	15 mL	butter
1 tablespoon	15 mL	vegetable oil
½ cup	125 mL	ketchup
¼ cup	50 mL	red wine vinegar
1 tablespoon	15 mL	Worcestershire sauce
1 tablespoon	15 mL	meat sauce*
2	2	whole cloves
2	2	bay leaves, crushed
1	1	garlic clove, minced
1 teaspoon	5 mL	salt
½ teaspoon	2 mL	pepper
1 cup	250 mL	red currant jelly

Preheat oven to 325°F (160°C).

Cut bird breasts in half. Mix eggs and water, dip breasts into mixture, then into bread crumbs. Brown in hot butter and oil. Place in casserole dish.

In bowl, combine ketchup, vinegar, Worcestershire sauce, meat sauce and remaining spices and seasonings (except jelly). Pour over meat and cover.

Bake for 2 to 3 hours or until tender, about 2 hours for duck, 2 to 3 hours for geese.

(Continued on next page.)

(Continued)

(The variability in cooking time is because it's next to impossible to know if the goose is young, grain-fed and tender or on the tough side. So allow lots of time for cooking – you may need it, and if not, the bird will hold once cooked.)

About 15 minutes before removing from oven, stir in jelly and let heat thoroughly.

Serves 6 to 8.

*Note: The meat sauce called for refers to H.P. sauce or A-1 sauce.

Pheasant in Wine

This recipe works equally well with partridge, prairie chicken, wild duck or pheasant. With the mushroom and wine sauce, it's a taste to savor!

2-3	2-3	birds, cut up*
½ cup	125 mL	butter
2 cups	500 mL	sliced mushrooms
1 cup	250 mL	dry white wine
2 tablespoons	30 mL	lemon juice
½ cup	125 mL	chopped green onions
1 teaspoon	5 mL	salt
		freshly ground pepper to taste

Preheat oven to 325°F (160°C) if you choose to oven bake.

Sauté bird in butter until lightly browned. Remove meat and sauté mushrooms in remaining butter. Return bird pieces to pan.

Add remaining ingredients, cover and simmer 1 to 1½ hours or until fork tender.

If you prefer to use oven, put ingredients into covered casserole and bake for 1 to 1½ hours or until fork tender.

To serve, arrange meat around wild rice on platter. Spoon juices over top.

Serves 6.

*Note: Cut birds into serving pieces or if birds are very small, use breasts only.

Jellied Apricot and Mandarin Orange Salad

2 x 3 ounces	2 x 85 g	apricot jelly powder
1 cup	250 mL	boiling water
1 cup	250 mL	orange juice
2 x 7 ½ ounces	2 x 213 mL	pureed apricots* (2 cans)
10 ounces	284 mL	mandarin orange sections
1 cup	250 mL	thinly sliced celery
⅓ cup	75 mL	finely chopped pecans
		orange segments and
		green cherries for garnish

Dissolve jelly powder in boiling water. Stir in orange juice and pureed apricots. Chill until slightly thickened.

Drain oranges and add with celery and pecans to jellied mixture. Pour into an attractive 6-cup (1.5 L) glass bowl or mold and chill until set.

If using mold, turn salad out onto lettuce-lined plate and garnish with additional orange segments and cherries. Or serve salad directly from its attractive bowl with garnish added on top.

Serves 10.

Note: You can puree canned apricots for this recipe or buy pureed apricots in the baby food section of the supermarket.

Notes

Halloween Party For Young and Old

In the early days, Halloween was a time of practical jokes, neighborhood tricks as well as costume parties and treating. Cities and towns were small and children could roam, scaring themselves and others with their tricks and costumes. Many Canadians can remember "soaping windows" and "tipping the outhouse". Everyone had to do it once – tip the schoolhouse outhouse or the one that belonged to the neighborhood grouch or the one with the lady inside it.

Today, such tricks are frowned upon and the "treat" part of Halloween has become the most important part for kids who, dressed in fancy costumes and with the biggest bag possible, go from house to house shouting "Trick or Treat". The more treats, the merrier.

Our menu includes a few treats for the kids but since they'll already have a bagful, we've also included some for the grown-ups. It's a nice way to end the day – with hot steaming coffee and tea for the adults, punch for the children and goodies for all.

Sometimes there are Halloween parties especially designed for adults. Guests are expected to arrive in costumes, the more outlandish the better – witches, ghosts, spacemen and monsters. Imagination has full reign. Entertainment generally includes games, guessing games, practical jokes, bobbing for apples in a pail of water to see who is quickest at bringing up an apple, and of course... good food!

MENU
● ● ● ●
Party Punch
Carmel Crunch Popcorn
Quick and Delicious Baked Doughnuts
Ginger Sparkles
Oatmeal Cookies... page 49
Cranberry Loaf... page 268
Steaming Hot Coffee and/or Tea

Party Punch

6 ounces	180 mL	frozen lemonade concentrate (1 can)
12 ounces	355 mL	orange juice concentrate (1 can)
2 x 32 ounces	2 L	ginger ale
		ice cubes or crushed ice

In a punch bowl or large pitcher, combine juices. At serving time add ale and ice.

Yields about 10 cups (2.5 L).

Baked Doughnuts

*Doughnuts were certainly a feature of many early Canadian kitchens
– some women made their culinary reputation with their splendid
doughnuts. Because the following version of doughnuts is baked, there
is less fuss and probably less fat. The best of both worlds!*

⅓ cup	75 mL	butter OR margarine
½ cup	125 mL	sugar
1	1	egg
1½ cups	375 mL	flour
2¼ teaspoons	11 mL	baking powder
¼ teaspoon	1 mL	salt
¼ teaspoon	1 mL	nutmeg
½ cup	125 mL	milk

Doughnut Dip:

½ cup	125 mL	melted butter
⅔ cup	150 mL	sugar
1½ teaspoon	7mL	cinnamon

Preheat oven to 350°F. (180°C)

Cream butter or margarine with sugar, add egg and mix well.
Combine dry ingredients and add alternately with milk to the creamed
mixture.

Fill small greased muffin cups half full. Bake for 20 to 25 minutes.

Roll warm doughnuts in melted butter, then roll in combined sugar
and cinnamon. Serve immediately or wrap in foil and reheat when
ready to serve.

If reheating, heat in 350°F (180°C) oven for about 15 minutes.

Yields about 30 doughnuts.

Ginger Sparkles

This is a basic molasses cookie, the kind that tastes best dipped in milk, tea or coffee. It's a dipper, in other words, delicious!

¾ cup	175 mL	shortening
1 cup	250 mL	sugar
1	1	egg
4 tablespoons	60 mL	molasses
1 teaspoon	5 mL	cinnamon
1¼ teaspoons	6 mL	ginger
2 cups	500 mL	flour
2 teaspoons	10 mL	baking soda
½ teaspoon	2 mL	salt
		granulated sugar to coat coolies

Preheat oven to 375°F (190°C).

Cream shortening and sugar, add egg and cream well. Add molasses and spices and mix well. Combine flour, baking soda and salt and add to first mixture.

Shape into small balls and roll in sugar to coat or shake in a bag. Place 2" (5 cm) apart on greased baking sheet and bake for about 10 minutes.

Yields about 50 cookies.

Oatmeal Cookies

Chewy, wholesome oatmeal cookies are a traditional snack across Canada, a legacy of the many Scottish settlers who loved oatmeal.

1¾ cups	425 mL	oatmeal
1½ cups	375 mL	flour
1 cup	250 mL	sugar
½ teaspoon	2 mL	baking soda
½ teaspoon	2 mL	salt
1 teaspoon	5 mL	cinnamon
1	1	egg, beaten
4 tablespoons	60 mL	milk
1 tablespoon	15 mL	molasses
½ cup	125 mL	melted shortening
½ cup	125 mL	melted butter
½ cup	125 mL	raisins

Preheat oven to 350°F (180°C).

In large mixing bowl, combine dry ingredients. In smaller bowl, combine egg, milk, molasses, shortening and butter. Add to dry ingredients and stir.

Stir in raisins. Drop by teaspoon on ungreased cookie sheet.

Bake for 12 to 14 minutes or until slightly browned.

Yields about 50 cookies.

Carmel Crunch Popcorn

There are 2 ways to go with this recipe. The cooked syrup can be poured over popped corn and nuts to make "Poppycock", a snack treat at any time. Or the syrup can be poured over the popcorn and the whole mass formed into popcorn balls, a traditional Halloween treat.

10 cups	2.5 L	popped corn
1⅓ cups	325 mL	sugar
½ cup	125 mL	butter OR margarine
½ cup	125 mL	corn syrup
1 teaspoon	5 mL	vanilla

Pop corn according to instructions on the container.

Place sugar, butter and corn syrup in saucepan over low heat, stirring constantly until mixture boils. Then boil quite rapidly, stirring frequently until syrup turns medium caramel color or until small amount dropped into cold water forms a hard, crisp ball, or until candy thermometer reads hard-ball stage (250-260°F {125°C}).

Add vanilla and remove from heat.

Pour syrup over popped corn, covering as many pieces as possible. Let cool slightly. Butter hands and form sticky popcorn into balls. Makes about 20-25 popcorn balls.

To make Poppycock, combine 8 cups (2 L) popped corn, 1 cup (250 mL) pecans and 1 cup (250 mL) unblanched toasted almonds.

Pour syrup over mixture and spread on greased cookie sheet. When cool break into chunks.

Candied Canadian Apples

Candied apples are a traditional Halloween treat in Canada. This old fashioned recipe produces a hard, sweet covering for the apple – expect it to last a long time.

10	10	eating apples
10	10	small sticks
2 cups	500 mL	sugar
½ cup	125 mL	light corn syrup
¾ cup	150 mL	water
8	8	drops red food coloring
1 teaspoon	5 mL	vanilla

Wash and dry apples, then insert stick into stem end. In small, deep saucepan, combine sugar, syrup and water.

Heat slowly, stirring until sugar dissolves. Then cook without stirring until mixture reaches the soft crack stage on candy thermometer, 275°F (135°C), or until small spoonful when dropped into cup of cold water turns hard and brittle. This process will take about 45 minutes.

Add food coloring and vanilla, and quickly dip apples into hot mixture.

Place coated apples upright on buttered tray so that a delicious shelf of candy forms on the top of the apple, with the stick at the bottom.

Notes

Christmas Eve Family Supper

For many Canadians, Christmas Eve is a family night. The kids are excited about the gifts, there is a church service to attend, last minute preparations to make for the following day, so the meal is generally simpler, something that can be made in advance and reheated when needed. That's why our menu for Christmas Eve features Steak and Kidney Pie, a memory-making dish in its own right!

The Réveillon menu in the Québec section, page 187, is a lovely menu for a Christmas season supper as well.

MENU
● ● ● ●

Beefsteak and Kidney Pie
Cranberry Chutney... page 65
Beet Pickles
Romaine and Orange Salad
Old English Fruit Trifle

Steak and Kidney Pie

This splendid buffet dish can be made the day before and refrigerated or even weeks before and frozen. The amount of kidney used depends on personal and family preferences, but even a small amount enhances the full-bodied flavor of this pie.

4 pounds	2 kg	lean stewing beef*
1-2	1-2	lamb kidneys
6 tablespoons	90 mL	beef fat OR lard
3	3	medium onions, diced
½ cup	125 mL	flour
2 x 10 ounces	2 x 284 mL	beef broth (2 cans)
1½ cups	375 mL	water
2 teaspoons	10 mL	prepared mustard
2 teaspoons	10 mL	Worcestershire sauce
2 teaspoons	10 mL	salt
1 teaspoon	5 mL	ground ginger
½ teaspoon	2 mL	cinnamon
½ cup	125 mL	red wine
2 cups	500 mL	sliced mushrooms
		pastry, page 165, enough to cover top of dish

Preheat oven to 450°F (230°C).

Cut beef in 1" (2.5 cm) pieces. Wash kidneys, remove membranes and cut into small pieces.

Melt fat or lard in heavy saucepan. Brown beef pieces. Remove and place in bowl.

Brown kidney and onions. Return beef to saucepan. Sprinkle flour over meat mixture and stir to brown slightly. Add beef broth, water, mustard, Worcestershire sauce, salt, ginger and cinnamon. Cover and simmer for about 1½ hours or until meat is fork tender.

(Continued on next page.)

(Continued)

Add red wine and mushrooms. Pour into greased 9 x 13" (3 L) baking dish.

Prepare pastry, recipe page 165. Roll thin. Moisten rim of baking dish and arrange pastry over top. Press edges firmly against sides and trim off extra pastry. Slit top for steam to escape.

Bake for 10 minutes. Lower heat to 357°F (190°C) and continue baking for 20 minutes or until crust is browned and filling bubbling hot.

Serves 8 to 10.

*Note: Beef from the cross rib or shoulder cut makes a tender meat pie. Round steak doesn't work as well.

Romaine and Orange Salad

This slightly tart, simple salad provides a good balance to the texture and flavor of a traditional dinner. Prepare everything ahead of time but toss the greens and dressing together just before serving.

1	1	large head romaine lettuce
3	3	oranges
¼ cup	50 mL	red wine vinegar
¾ cup	175 mL	salad oil
1 tablespoon	15 mL	honey
½ teaspoon	2 mL	salt
¼ teaspoon	1 mL	ground pepper
¼ cup	50 mL	chopped green onions

Rinse and dry lettuce on paper towels.

Store in plastic bag in refrigerator until crisp. (It's best if left for several hours or overnight.) Tear in bite-sized pieces.

Peel and slice the oranges. Shake vinegar, salad oil, honey, salt, pepper and green onions in a jar with lid.

Just before serving, put lettuce in a salad bowl. Sprinkle with dressing and toss.

Arrange orange slices on top and toss again.

Serves 10.

Beet Pickles

Traditionally, beet pickles were only made in the fall when the beets were ready for harvest. Then, the pickles turned up on tables all winter long, providing good taste, nutrition and a welcome dash of color. Now, with canned beets and this recipe, you can make beet pickles all year long.

2 x 14 ounces	2 x 398 mL	whole beets (2 cans)
1 cup	250 mL	beet juice
1 cup	250 mL	vinegar
¼ cup	50 mL	sugar
12	12	whole cloves

Drain beets and reserve juice. Place drained beets in two sterilized glass jars.

Combine beet juice, vinegar, sugar and cloves. Cover and bring to a boil and simmer for five minutes.

Pour over beets. Cover. Store in refrigerator until ready to use.

Old English Fruit Trifle

Elegant trifle desserts originated with settlers from the British Isles. As well as looking good and tasting even better, they can be made the day before and refrigerated. Layer ingredients in a deep, attractive glass bowl that holds about 8 to 10 cups (2 to 2.5 L).

Custard:

4 tablespoons	60 mL	cornstarch
4 tablespoons	60 mL	sugar
2 cups	500 mL	milk
3	3	eggs, beaten
1 teaspoon	5 mL	vanilla

Cake:

2	2	sponge cake layers*
¾ cup	175 mL	raspberry jam
⅓ cup	75 mL	Drambuie liqueur*
2 x 14 oz	2 x 398 mL	can sliced peaches*

Whipped Cream:

2 cups	500 mL	whipping cream
2 tablespoons	30 mL	sugar
2 teaspoons	10 mL	vanilla
		toasted almonds for garnish

Prepare custard first so it can cool while you assemble the rest of the trifle.

In small bowl, mix cornstarch and sugar to smooth paste with a little of allotted milk. Heat remainder of milk in heavy saucepan or double boiler. Stir in cornstarch paste and cook over very low heat, stirring constantly, until thick and smooth. Cook slowly for 3 to 4 minutes.

(Continued on next page.)

(Continued)

Remove from heat, add beaten eggs, 1 at a time. Return to heat, cook on low for 3 to 4 minutes. Remove from heat, add vanilla, and cool.

Cut cake layers in half. Spread with jam and put back together. Cut into cubes. Arrange half cake cubes in bottom of bowl. Sprinkle with half of Drambuie.

Drain canned peaches or prepare fresh ones. Arrange a layer of peaches over the cake. Spread half of cooled custard over peaches.

Whip cream until stiff. Fold in sugar and vanilla. Spread half the whipped cream over the custard layer.

Repeat layers of cake, Drambuie, peaches and custard. Top with whipped cream and garnish with toasted almond pieces.

Refrigerate overnight or at least for several hours.

Serves 8 to 10.

*Note: For convenience sake, you can buy sponge cake layers at the bakery or supermarket. You could also use the jelly roll base in Bûche de Noël, page 196. Instead of canned peaches, you can use four fresh peaches, peeled and sliced. Instead of Drambuie, you could use sherry.

Notes

Family Christmas Dinner

Christmas in Canada is a religious festival as well as a celebration of family and friends. Traditions include Christmas trees decorated with lights and ornaments. Christmas stockings on the mantelpiece, Santa Claus, who's supposed to do his best to fill those stockings... and a dinner table just groaning with the best possible food. Foods are traditional – turkey, goose, Tourtière, cranberry sauce – but there are also new foods as new cultural groups add their specialties to the Canadian mosaic.

The first suggested menu for Christmas Dinner is traditional; the second is a bit more daring. Both are genuinely Canadian and very, very good!

MENU
● ● ● ●

Traditional Roast Turkey
Sage Stuffing
Cranberry Chutney
Whipped Potatoes... page 75
Glazed Carrots and Onions... page 205
Broccoli Casserole
Plum Pudding
Hard Sauce OR
Rum Sauce... page 243
Marinated Oranges
Classic Fruit Cake... page 154
Classic Shortbread
Gingerbread Cookies

Traditional Roast Turkey

Christmas Day isn't complete in many Canadian homes without the smell of roasting turkey wafting through the house, just a hint of sage!

A 12 to 14 pound (5 to 6 kg) turkey will serve 12 large appetites with some left over for another day. To roast, allow about 20 minutes per pound. We've used 2 different kinds of stuffing in this recipe – a sage dressing to go in the main cavity and sausage meat dressing to go in the neck cavity. The sausage meat doesn't need any fixing – it's already spiced when you buy it in rolls in the frozen food section of the supermarket. Just put it into the neck cavity, close it securely and let it roast with the turkey. When it comes time to serve the bird, give everyone a thin slice of sausage meat along with the generous spoonful of sage stuffing… plus the turkey meat, of course. The three-way combination is very good.

12-14 pound	5-6 kg	turkey
1 pound	500 g	sausage meat

Sage Stuffing:

12 cups	3 L	dry bread crumbs
1 tablespoon	15 mL	dry sage
1½ teaspoon	7 mL	salt
		pepper to taste
¾ cup	175 mL	butter or margarine
1 cup	250 mL	chopped onion

Preheat oven to 325°F (160°C)

Wash and dry turkey.

Wrap giblets in foil and roast separately or put them beside the turkey about 2 hours before time to serve.

Put sausage meat into the neck cavity and sew the cavity closed or you can use skewers if you're careful.

To make the sage stuffing, crumble bread or buns, toss with sage, salt

(Continued on next page.)

(Continued)

and pepper. Melt butter or margarine in a saucepan and sauté onion until it is golden yellow. Drizzle over bread crumbs and toss lightly.

Stuff body cavity with bread crumb dressing. Sew shut with heavy thread or use skewers. If there is extra stuffing, drizzle a bit of pan juices over it, wrap in foil and bake for about an hour, serving along with the rest of the stuffing at serving time.

Place stuffed turkey in roasting pan breast side up. You may wish to tie the legs and wings to the body with heavy string. Cover lightly with foil, leaving sides open. Remove foil during last hour to brown.

Bake for about 5 hours. Baste occasionally with juices. Turkey is done when meat thermometer inserted into the center of the stuffing reaches 165°F (74°C).

You can also predict that a turkey is done when the drumsticks pull away from the body easily. When done, transfer turkey to a platter and cover with foil while finishing the gravy and vegetables.

Serves 12 or more.

Broccoli Casserole

For the green part of a special meal, why not try this make-ahead broccoli casserole? It's tasty, it looks good with its crumb/cheese topping and it can be served straight from the oven to the table.

2 pounds	1 kg	broccoli
¼ cup	50 mL	chopped onion
3 tablespoons	45 mL	butter
6 tablespoons	90 mL	flour
3 cups	750 mL	milk
1 cup	250 mL	shredded Cheddar cheese
½ cup	125 mL	cheese spread
1 teaspoon	5 mL	Worcestershire sauce
1 teaspoon	5 mL	salt
½ teaspoon	2 mL	freshly ground pepper
1 cup	250 mL	dry cracker crumbs
2 tablespoons	30 mL	melted butter

Preheat oven to 350°F (180°C).

Wash and coarsely chop broccoli. Cook until barely tender.

In the meantime, sauté onions in butter until tender. Stir in flour. Whisk in milk and cook until thickened, stirring frequently. Stir in cheese, cheese spread, Worcestershire sauce, salt and pepper.

Place drained broccoli in buttered casserole and pour sauce over top. Mix cracker crumbs and melted butter and sprinkle over cheese sauce.

Bake until crumbs are browned (about 15 minutes).

Cranberry Chutney

This Cranberry Chutney is splendid enough for the Christmas table and to bottle as gifts for special friends.

2 cups	500 mL	fresh OR frozen cranberries
1 cup	250 mL	sugar
½ cup	125 mL	water
1	1	large apple, peeled and chopped
½ cup	125 mL	raisins
½ teaspoon	2 mL	ground ginger

Wash cranberries. Combine with sugar, water, apple and raisins in a small saucepan.

Cover and simmer for about 15 minutes or until berries and apple are mushy. Stir in ginger.

Cool for several hours before serving.

Yields about 2 cups (500 mL).

Plum Pudding

Plum pudding has been a traditional Christmas dessert since the very earliest days when it was made from whatever could be scrounged – dried berries, imported fruits, barley, buffalo grease. It was somehow a symbol of survival in an alien land. Today, it lacks for nothing and is a symbol of happy times.

1½ cups	375 mL	raisins
1½ cups	375 mL	currants
1¼ cups	300 mL	brown sugar
1¼ cups	300 mL	suet OR butter
1 cup	250 mL	chopped dates
1 cup	250 mL	grated raw carrot
½ cup	125 mL	nuts (optional)
2 cups	00 mL	flour
1 teaspoon	5 mL	baking soda, salt, cinnamon EACH
½ teaspoon	2 mL	nutmeg, allspice EACH
2	2	eggs
2 tablespoons	30 mL	molasses
½ cup	125 mL	brandy, rum OR fruit juice
1	1	lemon, juice and rind

Preheat oven to 300°F (150°C) if using oven method.

Wash raisins and currants under hot, running water to plump them.

In large bowl, mix sugar with ground up suet, if you are using suet. To that mixture, add fruits and grated carrot.

If you are using butter, cream sugar and butter, flour and fruits slightly and add to the creamed mixture.

Fill an 8-cup (2 L) greased heat-proof bowl or mold or use 2 smaller greased pans. In either case, fill containers about ¾ full – allow for

(Continued on next page.)

some expansion. Cover top with foil or heavy cloth. Place on rack or trivet in large covered pot with 2 to 3" (5 to 7.5 cm) of water in bottom. Let pudding steam for 4 hours. Add more water if necessary.

Alternatively, you could use oven for this stage. Place the covered pudding in pan of water and bake for 3 to 4 hours.

Baking time depends on size of pan. Test for doneness.

Cool and wrap pudding in foil to ripen for several days, or freeze until needed.

To reheat place foil-wrapped pudding in 300°F (150°C) oven for 1 hour. Serve with Hard Sauce, page 68, or Rum Sauce, page 243.

Hard Sauce

Serve this classic topping for steamed Christmas pudding in an attractive glass serving bowl with a grating of nutmeg on top. Who can resist?

¾ cup	175 mL	butter
¾ cup	175 mL	icing (confectioner's) sugar
2 tablespoons	30 mL	brandy OR
1 teaspoon	5 mL	vanilla OR rum flavoring
2 teaspoons	10 mL	grated lemon rind
		grated nutmeg for garnish

Cream butter. Add sugar gradually, beating until mixture is light and fluffy.

Add brandy or vanilla or rum flavoring and lemon rind. Beat again.

Spoon into serving dish, grate nutmeg over top and chill.

Serves 10 to 12.

Marinated Oranges

Old-timers always recall the precious orange they got in the toe of their Christmas stocking years ago when oranges were few and far between. Now, we can get oranges year round, and serve them in wonderfully new ways.

Prepare this refreshing dessert several hours ahead of time and keep chilled until serving.

9	9	naval oranges
3 cups	750 mL	water
2 cups	500 mL	sugar
½ cup	125 mL	orange peel in strips
½ cup	125 mL	orange-flavored liqueur

Peel oranges, being sure to remove all of the white.

Slice oranges very thinly and remove seeds.

Bring water and sugar to a boil. Add orange peel and simmer until peel is shiny and transparent. Remove from heat, add liqueur. Pour over oranges and chill.

This dessert is very attractive, so show it off in a beautiful bowl. Serve in sherbet dishes.

Serves 8.

Classic Shortbread

Serving shortbread to visitors on New Year's Eve is an old-time custom among the Scots, one brought to Canada by early immigrants. Now it is a Canadian tradition to bake shortbread for all parties and gatherings during the Christmas season.

1 cup	250 mL	butter
⅔ cup	150 mL	icing (confectioner's) sugar
½ cup	125 mL	cornstarch OR rice flour
1¾ cups	425 mL	flour

Preheat oven to 300°F (150°C).

Cream butter until fluffy. Add sugar gradually and continue beating until sugar is completely dissolved. Stir in cornstarch or rice flour and regular flour.

Knead a few times until a smooth ball is formed.

Roll into small balls and flatten with a fork or cookie mold.

Or roll or pat to about ½" (1 cm) thickness. Cut in small fancy shapes with cookie cutters or arrange in a circle on cookie sheet, cut into wedges.

Bake for about 30 minutes or until very lightly browned.

Gingerbread Cookies

Gingerbread cookies turned up often in our foremothers' kitchens, partly because they were sturdy and lasted well. But also because they were a favorite with children, especially at Christmastime when they were iced and hung on the tree as decorations.

½ cup	125 mL	shortening
½ cup	125 mL	sugar
2	2	eggs
1 cup	250 mL	molasses
¼ cup	50 mL	water
3 cups	750 mL	flour
2 teaspoons	10 mL	ginger
1 teaspoon	5 mL	baking soda
½ teaspoon	2 mL	salt

Preheat oven to 350°F (180°C).

Cream shortening and sugar. Beat in eggs. Add molasses and water. Combine dry ingredients and stir in first mixture. Mix until smooth.

Roll out ⅓" (1 cm) thick and cut with cookie cutters or edge of a glass, or drop by spoonfuls and press down with floured tines of a fork.

Bake on greased cookie sheet for about 12 minutes or until lightly browned.

When cool, frost with small amount of butter icing. This is not absolutely necessary, but adds a delicious touch.

Notes

Christmas Dinner with A Difference

It was Dickens in his memorable "A Christmas Carol" who ensured the place of the goose on our Christmas tables. After Scrooge's visit with the ghosts of Christmas Past, Present and Future, he woke to a new day and sent a neighborhood boy down to get the fattest goose in the butcher's window – to take to the Cratchit's for their best Christmas ever!

Canadian pioneers had different reasons for choosing the goose for Christmas – often it was because wild geese were available and turkeys weren't – but goose still stars – for one reason or another – on our Christmas tables!

MENU
● ● ● ●

Roast Goose with Cranberry Topping
Whipped Potatoes
Turnip and Carrot Casserole
Dilled Green Beans
Pound Cake
Marinated Oranges... page 69
Classic Shortbread... page 70

Roast Goose with Cranberry Topping

Never mind all the jokes about your Christmas goose. This is too good to joke about!

8 pound	4 kg	goose, ready-to-cook
		salt and pepper
4 cups	1 L	cranberries
½ cup	125 mL	red currant jelly
¼ cup	50 mL	red wine vinegar
¼ cup	50 mL	red sweet wine
2 teaspoons	10 mL	Worcestershire sauce

Preheat oven to 400°F (200°C).

Thaw goose, if frozen. Rinse and drain. Place on a rack in shallow roasting pan and tie legs together.

Sprinkle with salt and pepper. Prick breast skin in several places with tines of fork so that fat can run out.

Roast uncovered for 1 hour. Reduce oven temperature to 325°F (160°C) and continue roasting for another 1½ hours or until meat thermometer inserted into thigh registers 185°F (85°C). Remove goose to platter.

Drain off fat and discard. Pour ½ cup (125 mL) water into pan and stir to dissolve and dislodge brown bits.

In the meantime, combine cranberries, jelly, vinegar, wine and Worcestershire sauce. Add to ½ cup (125 mL) liquid left in pan and simmer for about 5 minutes or until cranberries have just popped. Do not let mixture get mushy.

Pour over and around goose. Serve remaining sauce on the side.

Whipped Potatoes

Mashed potatoes are the traditional choice for Christmas Dinner – or any turkey dinner. This is a version that can be made in advance and then reheated at mealtime.

5 pounds	2.5 kg	potatoes (about 16)
1½ cups	375 mL	sour cream
2 teaspoons	10 mL	salt
1 teaspoon	mL	freshly ground pepper

Peel potatoes and boil in salted water. Drain and mash.

Add sour cream, salt and pepper and beat until smooth. Place in a lightly buttered casserole and refrigerated until needed.

Preheat oven to 350°F (180°C). Reheat (covered with foil) for about an hour. Or use microwave oven.

Serves 8.

Turnip and Carrot Casserole

There are folks who swear that a proper Christmas dinner must include turnips. There are other folks who aren't quite so keen on the noble turnip. This casserole is a nice compromise – the strength of the turnip is softened by the carrot, without losing all of its character.

2	2	medium turnips
2	2	large carrots
3 tablespoons	45 mL	butter
1 teaspoon	5 mL	salt
¼ teaspoon	1 mL	pepper
2	2	eggs, beaten
1½ cups	375 mL	bread crumbs
1½ tablespoons	25 mL	melted butter

Preheat oven to 350°F (180°C).

Cook turnips and carrots until tender. Drain well. Mash and drain again. Add butter, salt, pepper and beaten eggs.

Spoon into buttered casserole dish. Toss bread crumbs with melted butter and sprinkle over casserole.

Bake for 30 to 35 minutes or until casserole puffs.

You could make this in advance and refrigerate until about an hour before you plan to serve the meal. Then bake for about 1 hour.

Dilled Green Beans

This is a delicious way to serve green or wax beans. Try them hot for a winter dinner, cold for a summer picnic.

6-8 cups	1.5-2 L	green OR wax beans
		salt to taste
4 tablespoons	60 mL	butter OR margarine
1¼ teaspoons	7 mL	dried dill weed

Cook beans until just tender. Drain. Salt to taste.

Toss with butter and dill to coat evenly.

Note: You may use fresh or frozen beans.

Pound Cake

Nellie McClung, author and suffragette, wrote in her autobiography, that at all special occasions – teas, weddings, Christmas – "there had to be Pound Cake". It was a favorite of early days, partly because it was easy to make and store but also because it was tasty.

1 cup	250 mL	butter or margarine
1 cup	250 mL	berry sugar
1 tablespoon	15 mL	lemon juice
1 teaspoon	5 mL	salt
2 cups	500 mL	flour
4	4	eggs

Preheat oven to 350°F (180°C).

Cream butter or margarine. Add sugar and cream until light. Add lemon juice and salt. Beat until well blended.

Add flour gradually to creamed mixture, beating well after each addition. Beat in eggs one at a time.

Grease two 5 x 9" (12 x 22 cm) pans. Sprinkle with flour. Distribute batter evenly.

Bake for 1 hour or until lightly browned and a toothpick inserted into center comes out clean.

Let cool for 10 minutes, then invert onto cake rack.

The hardy pioneers did not ice this cake, but sometimes the younger generation like a bit of Lemon Butter icing, page 211.

Cherry Pound Cake

Measure 2 cups (500 mL) flour needed for Pound Cake (page 78), and remove 2 tablespoons (30 mL).

Chop 2 cups (500 mL) candied cherries and toss with the small amount of flour. Set aside.

Proceed with recipe as above, folding in floured cherries at the end.

Memories
"If a Sunday guest appeared we would serve a cup of tea, crackers and a bit of cheese, dark fruit cake or chocolate cake and partridgeberry tarts made from Grandma's old recipe."

Notes

New Year's Eve Midnight Supper

Canadians bring in the New Year with a bang-up party. Music, games, and a late supper lead up to midnight frivolities when everyone present forms a circle and joins hands to sing Auld Lang Syne.

On New Year's Day, the festivities continue with informal visiting as well as the more formal practice of "Open House".

We have lots of ideas for entertaining at this time of the year. You could share the work and organize a potluck dinner or you might take a leaf from the Alberta menu on page 235, and serve a Baron of Beef with breads, mustards, marinated onions and tomatoes – the basis of Hot Beef Sandwiches.

Or you might present a beautiful buffet – a groaning board, as early Canadians used to describe a generous display of food. We have included two menus for just such a choice.

MENU
● ● ● ●

Veal Terrine
Spiced Beef
Dilled Shrimp
Jellied Apricot and Mandarin Orange Salad... page 43
An assortment of breads and buns
Cranberry Sauce
Pickles, Dijon Mustard
Triple Chocolate Slice... page 26
Lemon Coconut Squares... page 24
Spiced Walnuts
Coffee and Tea

Veal Terrine

This terrine with its center of red cranberries is a festive sight, fun and delicious to have on a holiday buffet. Bake the terrine a day or so before your party.

2	2	eggs, slightly beaten
⅓ cup	75 mL	milk
1 tablespoon	15 mL	salt
1 tablespoon	15 mL	onion powder
1 tablespoon	15 mL	tarragon (optional)
3	3	bread slices, torn in pieces
3 pounds	1.5 kg	ground veal
1 cup	250 mL	thick cranberry sauce

Preheat oven to 350°F (180°C).

Combine eggs, milk, salt, onion powder and tarragon. Add bread and set aside for a few minutes to allow bread to soften.

Add half of veal and work with hands to combine well. Add remaining veal and work again with hands until mixture is well combined.

Pat half mixture into a 10-cup (2 L) loaf pan. Make shallow indentation in meat down length of pan.

Spread cranberries in hollow. Press remaining meat mixture over top. Pat firmly into place.

Bake for about 2 hours. Pour off any accumulated liquid. Let rest at least 15 minutes before unmolding.

For buffet, allow terrine to cool to room temperature, then wrap in foil or plastic wrap and chill thoroughly. At serving time, cut in thin slices and arrange on platter.

For other occasions, terrine may be served warm or at room temperature. If serving at table, unmold terrine and spread with additional Cranberry Sauce, page 85, or Cranberry Chutney, page 65.

Spiced Beef

For many Canadians, spiced beef – served on dark bread with mustard and pickles – is a Christmas treat. This is a quick and easy version of Spiced Beef that marinates in only 3-7 days instead of the weeks it used to take. When done, it will keep for a long time. You can also use buffalo or moose meat for this recipe – very Canadian and very tasty!

2 pounds	1 kg	flank steak
2 tablespoons	30 mL	sugar
½ teaspoon	2 mL	saltpeter
¾ teaspoon	3 mL	cloves, allspice, black pepper EACH

Preheat oven to 325°F (160°C).

Mix, sugar, saltpeter, spices and black pepper. Spread over meat on both sides.

Roll meat tightly and tie with a string.

Place in a heavy plastic bag in refrigerator for 3 to 7 days, turning every day to make certain the meat is thoroughly marinated.

Remove meat from marinade and wrap in foil. Place in roasting pan and bake for 2 hours.

Chill well before serving.

Serve on a cutting board or platter and slice very thinly.

Note: The flank steak should be about 1" (2.5 cm) thick. Saltpeter is available from a druggist.

Dilled Shrimp

You can serve these delicious shrimp as a salad already mixed and ready to go, or as a dip with the shrimp on the side. Either way, it's a terrific way to welcome a new year!

2 pounds	1 kg	large shrimp, cooked
1½ cups	375 mL	mayonnaise
⅓ cup	75 mL	lemon juice
¼ cup	50 mL	sugar
½ cup	125 mL	sour cream
1	1	large onion, finely chopped
2 tablespoons	30 mL	dried dill
½ teaspoon	2 mL	salt
		freshly ground pepper... and lots of it

Wash shrimp and keep refrigerated.

In large bowl, combine mayonnaise, lemon juice, sugar, sour cream, onion, dill, salt and pepper.

Refrigerate for several hours or overnight.

If serving as a dip, put into bowl surrounded by the shrimp. If serving as a salad, mix dressing with the shrimp, arrange in lettuce cups on salad plates.

Cranberry Sauce

Several varieties of cranberries – known variously as lingonberries, foxberries, partridgeberries – grow in muskegs and bogs across Canada and have been used for centuries to add flavor to our meals. Today, cranberries are grown commercially and turn up in all sorts of dishes... but the favorite remains the cranberry sauce that's served with turkey.

2 cups	500 mL	fresh OR frozen cranberries*
1 cup	250 mL	sugar
½ cup	250 mL	water
1 teaspoon	5 mL	grated orange peel, optional

Wash berries. Combine with sugar, water and orange peel in small saucepan and bring to a boil.

Simmer 8 to 10 minutes or until the skins of the cranberries begin to pop. Stir frequently.

Cool before serving.

Yields 1½ cups (375 mL).

*Note: if using frozen berries, increase cooking time to 20 to 25 minutes.

Spiced Walnuts

These are "good picking" to accompany port wine, fruit and cheese, or to come at the end of a special party. Try to get fresh walnuts – shell them yourself, if need be.

2 cups	500 mL	whole walnuts
2 tablespoons	30 mL	sugar
1 teaspoon	5 mL	cinnamon
¼ teaspoon	1 mL	allspice
¼ teaspoon	1 mL	mace
4 tablespoons	60 mL	butter OR margarine

Preheat oven to 325°F (160°C).

Toss nuts in mixture of sugar and spices. Melt butter or margarine and add to walnut mixture. Toss again.

Spread in single layer in shallow pan.

Bake for 10 minutes, stirring once while baking.

Store in covered container.

Holiday Open House Buffet

The Canadian custom of "paying a visit" sometime through the holiday season has evolved into more formal "Open House" arrangements, where food and drink are available all afternoon and evening and guests can "drop in" as they will.

The hostess of an "Open House" puts on her best bib and tucker, trying at once to serve food that tastes delicious but also looks terrific and lasts through a whole day's nibbling. Thus, our suggested menu includes recipes that are best suited to a buffet arrangement.

MENU
● ● ● ●

Holiday Eggnog
Veal Terrine... page 82
Spiced Beef... page 83
Dilled Shrimp... page 84
Rye Bread, Whole Wheat Bread, French Bread
Pickles and Dijon Mustard
Cranberry Chutney... page 65
Butter Tarts
Lemon Butter Tarts
Bakewell Tarts
Pork Pies, A Sweet Tart
Spiced Walnuts... page 86
Strong Fresh Coffee

Holiday Eggnog

Somehow, eggnog is just right for the Christmas season. Maybe it's all that cold weather out there, or maybe it's just a symbol of hospitality, but whatever – it's much appreciated and always delicious.

6	6	eggs, separated
¼ cup	50 mL	sugar
½ cup	125 mL	sugar
2 cups	500 mL	light cream
2 cups	500 mL	milk
½ cup	125 mL	rum
½ cup	125 mL	brandy
1 cup	250 mL	whipping cream
		nutmeg to sprinkle
		on top of the eggnog

Separate eggs. In large bowl, beat the whites to soft peak stage. Gradually add the ¼ cup (50 mL) sugar, continuing to beat until egg whites are stiff.

In another large bowl, beat egg yolks until light, then gradually add the ½ cup (125 mL) sugar.

Stir in light cream, milk, rum and brandy. Whip cream and fold into egg yolk mixture.

Finally, fold in the egg whites. Chill. To serve, sprinkle with nutmeg.

Serves about 12 people.

Lemon Butter Tarts

*These tarts should be tiny – just big enough for a delectable mouthful!
Bake the tart shells ahead of time or buy them and fill at the last
minute.*

1 teaspoon	5 mL	grated lemon rind
6 tablespoons	90 mL	lemon juice
¼ cup	50 mL	butter
2	2	large eggs, beaten
1 cup	250 mL	sugar

Wash and dry 16 ounce (500 mL) glass jar. Keep it warm to receive the lemon filling when it's done.

Grate lemon rind very finely, and squeeze juice.

Place rind, juice, butter, eggs and sugar in top of double boiler or in saucepan set in a pan of water.

Simmer water on low heat for 15 to 20 minutes until the mixture thickens. Don't let it boil.

Pour into warmed jar.

Chill and spoon into baked tart shells to form lemon-butter tarts. Can also be used as a filling for cakes or jelly roll.

Lemon Butter will keep in the refrigerator for up to 6 weeks if tightly covered.

Bakewell Tarts

*The combination of pastry, jam and cake in this tart is delicious,
unusual and surprisingly not too sweet.*

		as much pastry as would be needed for a 2-crust pie raspberry OR strawberry jam
1 cup	250 mL	butter
1 cup	250 mL	sugar
2	2	eggs
1 teaspoon	5 mL	vanilla
1½ cups	375 mL	flour
2 teaspoons	10 mL	baking powder
¼ teaspoon	1 mL	salt
½ cup	125 mL	milk OR water

Preheat oven to 400°F (200°C).

Lightly butter about 36 tart tins – 3" (7 cm) in diameter, and line with pastry. Spread jam in bottom of each tart shell, about ¼" (5 mm) in depth.

Cream butter and sugar. Add eggs and vanilla. Beat.

Mix dry ingredients together and add to the creamed mixture alternately with the milk or water.

Spoon a heaping teaspoon of batter on top of jam in tart shell.

Bake for 10 to 15 minutes or until lightly browned and pastry is cooked.

Butter Tarts

Butter tarts are greeted enthusiastically all over Canada. In parts of eastern Canada, cooks substitute maple syrup for part of the sugar whereas prairie cooks use part corn syrup.

		enough pastry for 14-16 tarts
½ cups	125 mL	raisins OR currant
3 tablespoons	45 mL	soft butter
½ cup	125 mL	brown sugar
¾ cup	175 mL	corn syrup
1	1	egg
¼ teaspoon	1 mL	salt

Preheat oven to 400°F (200°C).

Line 14-16 medium-sized muffin tins or tart tins with pastry, recipe page 165.

Rinse raisins or currants with boiling water and pat dry with a towel.

With a fork, mix butter, sugar, syrup, egg and salt. Add raisins or currants and mix well.

Spoon mixture into unbaked shells, no more than ⅔ full. Place oven rack below center of oven so that pastry will bake before the filling burns.

Bake tarts for 15 to 20 minutes or until pastry is golden and filling is puffy. Cool in tins until tarts are firm enough to remove without crumbling.

Pork Pies, A Sweet Tart

Don't let the unusual name fool you. These are lovely looking, delicious little tarts that originated in the Acadian region of Canada. The pastry shells can be made ahead and frozen.

Tart Shells:

1 cup	250 mL	butter OR margarine
4 tablespoons	60 mL	icing (confectioner's) sugar
2 cups	500 mL	flour

Tart Filling:

2 cups	500 mL	cut up dates
1 cup	250 mL	water
¾ cup	175 mL	brown sugar

Topping:

¼ cup	50 mL	butter OR margarine
1 cup	250 mL	icing (confectioner's) sugar
		milk, if needed,
		to moisten icing
1 teaspoon	5 mL	maple flavoring

Preheat oven to 325°F (160°C).

Mix butter or margarine with icing sugar and flour. Press into tart shells. Bake for about 15 minutes or until lightly browned. Cool before removing from pan.

To make date filling, cook dates, water and brown sugar over low heat until thick and mushy. Use small amount to fell each tart shell.

To make the topping, cream the butter or margarine with icing sugar, adding milk if needed. Add maple flavoring.

Using a cake decorator put a rosette of icing on top of each tart, or simply spoon a mound on each tart.

Midwinter Madness

Midwinter madness strikes Canadians between January and April, propelling us all outdoors to make the best of the winter weather. Thus, Ottawa organizes the annual Winterlude with skating on the Rideau Canal. Whitehorse runs dogsled and snowshoe races at their Sourdough Rendezvous. Other cities and towns organize skating carnivals, winter festivals, curling bonspiels and winter fests of every variety.

Most famous of all is the Québec Winter Carnival, a celebration of winter if ever there was one... snow sculpturing, snowmobile races, hockey, curling, broomball, ice fishing, snowshoeing and a rollicking good time keep home town folks and visitors busy for 10 days. On the second Saturday of the Carnival, and Alberta contingent arrives to make the famous open-air Stampede breakfast – pancakes, bacon and coffee. So, our midwinter madness menu includes both East and West – it's a mix-n-match meal for Midwinter!

MENU
● ● ● ●
French Canadian Ragout
Romaine and Orange Salad... page 56
French Bread
Hot Gingerbread with Sweetened Whipped Cream... page 174
Classic Chili
Baked Cherry Tomatoes
Cornbread, page 118
Quick Whole Wheat Loaf... page 14
Carrot Cake with Cream Cheese Icing... page 124
Chuckwagon Pancakes
Maple Syrup
Bacon
Spoon-Dissolving Coffee

French Canadian Ragout

A full-bodied ragout is one of the finest French Canadian dishes. This particular recipe calls for beef, but it could also be made with buffalo, moose or other Canadian wild game. Serve in a deep casserole. Delicious with noodles and a green salad.

1½ pounds	750 g	beef cut in cubes
½ cup	125 mL	four
		freshly ground pepper
2 tablespoons	30 mL	butter
2 tablespoons	30 mL	vegetable oil
2	2	medium onions, chopped
3	3	carrots, cubed
2	2	celery stalks, sliced
10 ounces	284 mL	beef consomme (1 can)
1 cup	250 mL	canned tomatoes
1 tablespoon	15 mL	sugar
2 teaspoons	10 mL	salt
		freshly ground pepper
½ teaspoon	2 mL	oregano
1 cup	250 mL	small green peas*

Preheat oven to 350°F (150°C).

Dredge the beef cubes in mixture of flour and pepper. In heavy saucepan, brown floured beef cubes in butter and vegetable oil. Remove to large casserole.

Brown onion in remaining butter and oil. Add to meat mixture.

Add remaining ingredients to meat mixture, except for the peas.

Cover and bake for 2 hours or until meat is tender. Some stew meats

(Continued on next page.)

(Continued)

take longer than others to tenderize.

If ragout is too thin at this point, mix 3 tablespoons (45 mL) cornstarch with ½ cup (125 mL) water, mix well and stir in as much as needed to thicken ragout juices. Add peas and bake for 5 to 10 minutes.

(If you are uncertain of the quality of the beef and the cooking time, cook the ragout ahead of time. It reheats very well – some say it tastes better.)

Serve with noodles and a green salad.

Serves 4.

*Note: Use fresh, frozen or canned green peas.

Classic Chili

The chili debate goes on elsewhere, but in Canada, chili is traditionally made with kidney beans, meat and tomatoes. Some like it hot, some prefer a little less chili powder. Take your pick!

1½ pounds	750 g	ground beef
1¼ cups	300 mL	chopped onions
28 ounces	796 mL	red kidney beans
28 ounces	796 mL	tomatoes
2-3 tablespoons	30-45 mL	chili powder
1 tablespoon	15 mL	flour
1 teaspoon	5 mL	salt
		dash freshly ground pepper
		dash cumin

In large skillet, break up beef and cook until lightly browned. Remove to bowl.

In remaining fat, sauté onion until soft. Put beef back into pan and add remaining ingredients.

Simmer over low heat for about 30 minutes, stirring occasionally.

Serve chili piping hot and offer 1 or more of the following accompaniments along with it: sour cream, grated cheese, fresh chopped tomatoes, chopped green onions.

Serves 4 to 6.

Note: Whole canned tomatoes work well for chili. As liquid may vary from can to can, keep part of the tomato juice until you're certain that you need it.

Baked Cherry Tomatoes

Tomatoes just had to be invented – if not for their flavor, then for their color. They add instant sparkle to a plate, instant taste to the palate.

2-3	2-3	cherry tomatoes, per person
		salt, freshly ground pepper
		and basil to taste

Preheat oven to 350°F (180°C).

Make a cross in top of each cherry tomato.

Arrange in a casserole with cross at top. Sprinkle with salt, pepper and basil.

Bake for 10 to 15 minutes or until tomatoes are soft but not mushy.

Chuckwagon Pancakes

Pancakes – also known as hot cakes and flapjacks – were and still are a staple across Canada. Many are the bachelor rancher or farmer who survived on plain old pancakes until he found himself a wife, or a restaurant!

With such fond memories, it's no wonder that pancakes turn up at various community celebrations whether served from a chuckwagon at the Calgary Stampede or out at the cottage when neighbors come calling!

This particular recipe is a favorite of Western historian, Grant MacEwan.

1 cup	250 mL	flour
¼ cup	50 mL	whole-wheat flour
¼ cup	50 mL	cornmeal
1 tablespoon	15 mL	baking powder
1 teaspoon	5 mL	sugar
½ teaspoon	2 mL	salt
⅓ cup	75 mL	vegetable oil*
2	2	eggs, beaten
1½ cups	375 mL	milk
		butter OR vegetable oil to grease the pan

In large bowl, combine flours, cornmeal, baking powder, sugar and salt. Make a well in center and add oil, eggs and milk. Beat well. Let set for a few minutes so that the batter thickens and puffs.

Heat heavy frying pan or griddle, grease slightly. Pour about ⅓ cup (75 mL) batter onto the hot surface. When pancake is bubbly, turn and cook other side.

Serve with maple syrup, fruit syrup, jam or jelly.

(Continued on next page.)

(Continued)

For a really hearty meal, serve up with sausages and/or bacon, scrambled eggs, even steak.

Buckwheat Pancakes: Buckwheat pancakes, considered to be a specialty of New Brunswick, can be made by substituting ½ cup (125 mL) buckwheat for the whole-wheat flour and cornmeal.

Traditional Pancakes: A lighter pancake can be made by using white flour only, thus using in total 1½ cups (375 mL) white all-purpose flour.

Blueberry Pancakes: This Maritime specialty can be made by adding ½ cup (125 mL) blueberries to the Traditional Pancake batter on page 98.

Apple Pancakes: Add thinly sliced, peeled and cored apple to the Traditional Pancake batter, above, making sure that an apple slice is placed in the center of each pancake as it is cooked on the griddle.

*Note: Instead of the vegetable oil, you could use melted butter or margarine.

Notes

A Sugaring Off
with Maple Syrup Treats

Sugar maple treats grow in Québec, Ontario and the Maritime Provinces. When spring comes with its cold clear nights and warm sunny days, the sap in the trees begins to run and everyone knows that it's time for "sugaring off".

It started with native Indians. When white men first came to sugar bush country, they saw them boil sweet sap from the maple trees to produce wonderfully sweet granular maple syrup. For the Indians, "sugaring off" was a time of merriment, a celebration of the end of winter and the return of growth and life.

Although today's sugaring operations are mechanized, the mood of fun and celebration has survived. Generally, visitors are welcomed at the Sugar Shacks and are given a treat – hot thick syrup spread on clean snow. As it hardens, the candy is twisted around a wooden stick or spoon and enjoyed on the spot.

The work season is apt to end with a Sugaring Off party at which most everything contains maple syrup… Ham Glazed with Maple Syrup, Baked Beans sweetened with Maple Syrup, Dumplings simmered in Maple Syrup, Maple Syrup Pie, Maple Syrup Tarts and Maple Parfait. Truly a celebration food of Canada!

MENU
● ● ● ●
Maple Mousse
Dumplings in Maple Syrup
Maple Syrup Pie
Maple Tarts Forever
Maple Parfait
Sugar on Snow

Maple Mousse

This light creamy dessert is so "Canadian" that it's often served at official government banquets.

1 tablespoon	15 mL	gelatin (1 envelope)
¼ cup	50 mL	cold water
1¾ cups	425 mL	maple syrup
4	4	eggs, separated
2 cups	500 mL	whipping cream

Soften gelatin in cold water.

In heavy saucepan or double boiler, combine maple syrup and egg yolks. Gently simmer for 5 minutes, stirring frequently.

Add softened gelatin and stir until dissolved. Cool until just beginning to thicken.

In the meantime, whip egg whites until they stand in stiff peaks and whip cream until stiff and smooth.

Fold egg whites into maple syrup mixture, then fold in whipped cream.

Pour into an attractive glass bowl so that you can serve right from bowl into individual serving dishes.

Cover and chill thoroughly for at least 3 hours.

If desired, garnish with rosettes of whipped cream or low-calorie topping.

Serves 8.

Dumplings in Maple Syrup

Known as Grandpères in French Canada, this children's favorite is a great comfort food – warm, chewy, sweet, tasting of home and good times.

		dumpling batter, same as doughboys, page 183
2 cups	500 mL	maple syrup

Prepare dumpling batter according to recipe for doughboys on page 183. Omit parsley.

In deep frying pan or saucepan, bring maple syrup to a boil. Reduce heat and simmer until slightly thickened.

Drop small spoonfuls of batter into simmering maple syrup. Cover and cook for about 15 minutes.

Turn the dumplings and cook for another 10 minutes or so.

Serve as a dessert with Sweetened Whipped cream, page 35, or with the Homemade Vanilla Ice cream, page 15.

Maple Syrup Pie

Maple Syrup Pie has as many names as it has variations! In Québec, it's known as Tarte au Sirop d'Erable; in New Brunswick, it's sometimes called Backwoods Pie; in other parts of Canada, it's known simply as Maple Syrup Pie. Always it is known as delicious!

		pastry for a single 8 OR 9" (20-23 cm) pie shell
1½ cups	375 mL	maple syrup
⅓ cup	75 mL	flour
½ cup	125 mL	water
½ cup	125 mL	light cream
1 tablespoon	15 mL	butter
1 teaspoon	5 mL	vanilla
⅓ cup	75 mL	walnuts OR pecans

Preheat oven to 350°F (180°C).

Prepare pastry, page 165. Line bottom of pie plate. Bring syrup to boil in heavy saucepan.

In small bowl, combine flour and water. Spoon in a bit of hot syrup, mix well, then pour back into hot syrup. Mix well.

If there are any lumps, put through strainer. Add cream. Simmer 5 minutes, stirring constantly.

Remove from heat. Add butter and vanilla. Pour into pie shell.

Chop nuts and sprinkle in a circle around the outside edge of pie. Bake for 25 minutes or until shell edge is browned.

Serve with Sweetened Whipped cream, page 35. Since this pie is so rich, cut into small wedges.

Serves 8.

Maple Tarts Forever

		enough pastry to fill 12 small tart tins
2	2	eggs
½ cup	125 mL	sugar
1 cup	250 mL	maple syrup

Preheat oven to 425°F (220°C).

Prepare pastry according to recipe on page 165. Or use frozen pie shell.

Beat eggs until just mixed. Stir in sugar until dissolved.

Add maple syrup, stirring as little as possible. This keeps filling from boiling over during baking.

Spoon into pastry-lined tart shells.

Bake for 10 to 15 minutes until pastry is lightly browned.

Cool in tins until tarts are firm enough to remove without crumbling.

Maple Parfait

This simple Canadian dessert has the elegance and taste to finish off the most important celebration.

maple syrup, enough to cover
the ice cream
vanilla ice cream, enough to
hold the maple syrup

Bring maple syrup to a boil. Place small scoops of ice cream into parfait glasses or sherbet dishes.

Spoon hot syrup over top.

Sugar on Snow

This recipe harkens back to the good old days when the person in charge of boiling the maple syrup would test the results by dribbling a bit on a nearby snowdrift. Kids would of course fight for the tasting rights. When the syrup was just right, it would harden on the snow. Then it could be twisted around a wooden spoon or stick and enjoyed on the spot... by children and adults alike!

To approximate "sugar on snow" in our modern kitchens, take about 4 cups (1 L) maple syrup and bring to a boil in heavy saucepan.

Cook until candy thermometer reaches 240°F (115°C).

While the syrup boils, get the kids to collect clean snow in bowls. When syrup is ready, dribble it over the snow. The candy will set almost immediately so you can eat at once.

Easter Sunday Dinner

Easter is primarily a Christian religious festival but it also connotes spring – a new birth, a new season, a time to celebrate. Families get together, kids eat more chocolate than they should... and everyone has a lovely time!

Typically, baked ham or roast leg of lamb is served at Easter and we have featured the latter in the menu that follows. However, if you'd like to serve ham for Easter, use the Saskatchewan dinner menu on page 225.

MENU
● ● ● ●
Roast Leg of Lamb
Mint Sauce
Delectable Rice OR Spinach Rice Bake
Dilled Green Beans... page 77
Sweet and Sour Carrot Salad
Old English Fruit Trifle... page 58 OR
Lemon Meringue Pie... page 162

Roast Leg of Lamb

A standard leg of lamb should serve about 8 people. Directions are given for both rare and well-done lamb, but most Canadians like their lamb well-done.

1	1	leg of lamb
1	1	garlic clove, slivered
1 teaspoon	5 mL	rosemary
		salt and freshly ground
		pepper to taste
10 ounces	284 mL	beef broth (1 can)
4 tablespoons	60 mL	Madeira wine (optional)

Preheat oven to 325°F (160°C).

Cut small slits in outer skin of lamb and insert slivers of garlic.

Sprinkle with rosemary, salt and pepper. Place on rack in roasting pan and roast uncovered for about 35 minutes per pound (70 minutes per kg).

Use meat thermometer for precision; it should read 170°F (75°C) for well-done or 140°F (65°C) for rare.

When done, transfer lamb to platter. Remove most of fat from roasting pan and discard.

Add beef broth and wine to remaining fat, heat and stir. Serve sauce in gravy boat and spoon over slices of lamb.

Note: You may use port wine in place of the Madeira or you can leave the wine out entirely.

Mint Sauce

Mint Sauce made from scratch has a freshness that makes preparing it worthwhile.

1 tablespoon	15 mL	dried mint
4 tablespoons	60 mL	cider vinegar
1 teaspoon	5 mL	sugar
1	1	small green onion, chopped

Crush mint in vinegar until vinegar is dark green.

Add sugar and onion.

Let sit for several hours before using.

Delectable Rice

This rice en casserole can be served on many occasions. If it's going to accompany beef, use beef broth. If it's to be with poultry or ham, use chicken broth. It can be made ahead and reheated.

⅓ cup	75 mL	butter OR margarine
½ cup	125 mL	chopped onion
2 cups	500 mL	long-grain rice
2 x 10 ounce	2 x 284 mL	chicken broth (2 cans)
2½ cups	625 mL	water
1½ teaspoons	7 mL	salt
¼ teaspoon	1 mL	curry powder
3-4 tablespoons	45-60 mL	chopped parsley

Preheat oven to 350°F (180°C).

Put butter or margarine in frying pan and sauté onion until soft. Add remaining ingredients, except parsley and stir.

Place in a 2-quart (2 L) casserole dish. Cover and bake for about 1 hour. Stir once or twice during baking period. Before serving, sprinkle with chopped parsley.

Serves 8 to 10.

Spinach Rice Bake

Serve this delicious casserole with ham, beef or lamb. It's perfect to take to a potluck – easily portable, needing only to be popped into the oven once you arrive at the host home.

4 cups	1 L	cooked rice
4	4	eggs
1 cup	250 mL	milk
2 tablespoons	30 mL	finely chopped onions
1 tablespoon	15 mL	Worcestershire sauce
2 teaspoons	10 mL	salt
1 cup	250 mL	grated Cheddar cheese
¼ teaspoon	1 mL	thyme
¼ teaspoon	1 mL	marjoram
10 ounces	300 g	frozen spinach
¼ cup	50 mL	butter to dot casserole

Preheat oven to 350°F (180°C).

Prepare rice according to package instructions.

Beat eggs until light. Add milk, onion, Worcestershire sauce, salt, cheese, thyme and marjoram.

Cook spinach according to package instructions, drain well and press out excess liquid. Chop coarsely.

Add spinach and rice to egg mixture. Pour into buttered casserole dish. Dot with butter.

Bake for 45 minutes or until set.

Sweet and Sour Carrot Salad

This interesting blend of sweet and sour is best made a day ahead, and refrigerated to blend the flavors. You may serve it hot or cold... but be sure to serve it often!

2 pounds	1 kg	carrots
1	1	green pepper
1	1	medium onion, sliced

Marinade:

10 ounces	284 mL	tomato soup (1 can)
¾ cup	175 mL	vinegar
⅓ cup	75 mL	vegetable oil
¾ cup	175 mL	sugar
1 teaspoon	5 mL	prepared mustard
1 teaspoon	5 mL	Worcestershire sauce
1 teaspoon	5 mL	salt
		pepper to taste

Preheat oven to 350°F (180°C).

Peel carrots and cut crosswise in thin rounds. Simmer in salted water for 10 minutes or until just tender-crisp. Drain. Cover with ice water and drain again.

Slice green pepper into thin strips and add with sliced onion to carrots.

Mix remaining ingredients in jar and shake well. Pour over vegetables.

If you wish to serve vegetables cold, refrigerate at this point for at least 24 hours.

If you'd rather have your vegetables hot, place vegetable mixture into greased baking dish and bake for about 30 minutes or until mixture is heated through.

Serves 8 to 10.

Brunch at the Cottage

Canadians have always liked to visit on the weekends. In early times, before radio and telephones, visiting provided a way of keeping up with the news. In more modern times, with news coming at us from all technological sides, visiting provides the personal touch, the friendships that technology can't buy!

Which is why weekend brunches have become a favorite way of entertaining. The following suggested menu is pretty straightforward – eggs and sausage with a selection of quick breads, just like grandma might have served – except that the sausages are new and different, the eggs are visitor friendly and the quick breads combine the best of old and new!

MENU
● ● ● ●

Orange Juice Flip
Sausage Balls
Oven Cheese Omelet
Sliced Tomatoes with Basil
Cornbread or Cornmeal Muffins
Oatmeal Muffins
Red Currant Jelly
Lemon Marmalade
Fresh Fruit Tray
Almond Shortcake... page 139

Orange Juice Flip

This fresh frothy orange drink looks and tastes marvelous. Serve in wine goblets or old-fashioned glasses.

12 ounces	355 mL	orange juice concentrate
1½ cups	375 mL	milk
½ cup	125 mL	water
2 tablespoons	30 mL	sugar
1½ teaspoons	7 mL	vanilla
12	12	ice cubes
1 cup	250 mL	water

Place all ingredients, except the last 1 cup (250 mL) water, in blender and blend until ice cubes have been finely ground.

Blend in remaining water – being careful not to let liquid overflow the blender.

Serves 8.

Sausage Balls

These specially seasoned sausage balls are delicious for a breakfast or brunch. They can be baked ahead and reheated, or baked, frozen and reheated.

1 pound	500 g	ground pork
1 pound	500 g	sausage meat
3	3	bread slices
¼ cup	50 mL	milk
2 teaspoons	10 mL	salt
2 teaspoons	10 mL	sage
¾ teaspoon	3 mL	freshly ground pepper
1 teaspoon	5 mL	coriander
½ teaspoon	2 mL	dry mustard
½ teaspoon	2 mL	nutmeg

Preheat oven to 350°F (180°C).

Combine ground park and sausage meat.

Break bread into pieces and soak in milk until mushy. Add seasonings to bread mixture, mix briefly.

Add to meat mixture and mix thoroughly.

Roll into 2" (5 cm) balls. Place in baking dish, making sure they do not touch.

Bake about 60 minutes or until lightly browned and no longer pink.

Turn once during baking. If sausage balls are not brown enough, place under broiler for a few minutes.

Serve immediately, or freeze until needed. If reheating, give them about 20 minutes at a low temperature.

Yields 16 generous sausage balls or 8 to 10 servings.

Note: You can find sausage meat in the frozen food section of the supermarket. It comes already seasoned.

Oven Cheese Omelet

This oven omelet is a foolproof, delicious and congenial way of serving eggs for a brunch. Put the omelet into the oven when the guests arrive and it will be obligingly ready as soon as the guests have had their orange juice starter!

10	10	eggs
1 ⅓ cups	325 mL	milk
1 teaspoon	5 mL	salt
¼ teaspoon	1 mL	freshly ground pepper
1 teaspoon	5 mL	dried parsley
2 cups	500 mL	grated Cheddar cheese

Preheat oven to 350°F (180°C).

Beat eggs until well blended. Add remaining ingredients and mix lightly. Pour mixture in a lightly battered 9 x 13" (23 x 33 cm) baking dish.

Bake for about 35 minutes or until puffy and lightly browned.

Serve immediately if you want the omelet to look its best. Otherwise, the eggs will settle a bit...but they'll still taste terrific.

Serves 6 to 8.

Sliced Tomatoes with Basil

Select blemish-free field tomatoes.

Cut crosswise in thick even slices and arrange on a serving plate.

Sprinkle lightly with salt, pepper and basis – either chopped fresh or dried. (Use about twice as much fresh as dried. Adjust to taste).

Drizzle store-bought red wine vinaigrette over tomatoes just before serving.

Cornbread or Cornmeal Muffins

Settlers in the New England states learned about corn from the Indians around them, and cornbread became one of their staple dishes. It was also known as Johnny Cake or Journey Cake, and when the Loyalists from New England journeyed to Canada, they brought their Journey Cake along.

1½ cups	375 mL	cornmeal
2½ cups	625 mL	buttermilk
2	2	eggs, beaten
½ cup	125 mL	vegetable oil
⅔ cup	150 mL	sugar
2 cups	500 mL	flour
1 tablespoon	15 mL	baking powder
1 teaspoon	5 mL	baking soda
2 teaspoons	10 mL	salt

Preheat oven to 400°F (200°C).

Combine cornmeal with buttermilk, eggs, oil and sugar and set aside for 10 minutes. Cornmeal will soften somewhat.

Mix dry ingredients. Fold into cornmeal mixture, stirring only until blended.

Spread into greased 9 x 13" (23 x 33 cm) cake pan or into approximately 14 greased muffin cups.

Bake for about 30 minutes for cake, 15 to 20 minutes for muffins.

Test with toothpick.

Oatmeal Muffins

This recipe makes 12 light tender muffins, suitable for breakfast for brunch or most any other occasion when you feel the need of a tasty snack!

1 cup	250 mL	oatmeal
1 cup	250 mL	buttermilk
¼ cup	50 mL	melted shortening
¼ cup	50 mL	brown sugar
1	1	egg, beaten
1 cup	250 mL	flour
½ teaspoon	2 mL	salt
2½ teaspoons	12 mL	baking powder
½ teaspoon	2 mL	baking soda

Preheat oven to 400°F (200°C).

Combine oatmeal with buttermilk. Add melted shortening, sugar and egg. Mix briefly.

Mix remaining dry ingredients and add to mixture, stirring only to moisten.

Spoon into 10 to 12 greased muffin tins, filling each about ⅔ full.

Bake for 20 minutes or until lightly browned.

Makes 12.

Notes

Corn Roast and/or Wiener Roast

Canadians don't get as much summer as some people in this world, so we get busy and celebrate it when it comes! One of the best outdoor summer recreations is a Wiener Roast or Corn Roast or both! All that's needed is the great outdoors, a bonfire, willow sticks to hold the wieners as they roast, and a pot full of hot water to cook fresh corn.

You may want to add a salad and dessert to your Wiener/Corn Roast or you may want to stick to the basics. It's up to you!

MENU

● ● ● ●

Hot Dogs
Mustard, Relish
Chopped Onions and Tomatoes
Cheese Slices or Cheese Spread
Fresh Corn on The Cob
Butter, Salt and Pepper
Caesar Salad... page 130
Carrot Cake with Cream Cheese Icing
Nanaimo Bars
Roasted Marshmallows

Hot Dogs

Most people know how to make hot dogs but some may not know how to make them the original Canadian way. For that, you need a bonfire and a willow stick. Thread the cold wiener on the willow stick, hold it over the fire (not in the flame unless you want the charbroiled effect) until it sizzles and then pop it into a prepared bun. Keep the willow stick – you'll need it for roasting the marshmallows – another must for a wiener roast!

If you're boiling your wieners, you can cut through the skin on one side of the wiener. As it boils, it will curl around and you can make a round hot dog. Use a hamburger or other round bun. Finish with the usual condiments.

You can also spoon hot chili over your wiener in the bun and thus create a chili dog. Have lots of paper napkins on hand!

Two Ways with Corn

The most important ingredient of any corn roast is the freshest corn you can get. With that, you can roast the corn or boil it.

Boiled Corn: To boil, fill a large kettle with water and set over a fire, bonfire or stove. While the water is coming to a boil, remove the husks from the corn. As soon as the water is boiling vigorously, add the corn, 1 teaspoon (5 mL) salt and return to a simmering boil. Simmer for about 7 minutes.

Have a bowl of melted butter ready to brush on the corn, or put out chunks of butter so that the guests can twirl their cobs through the butter themselves. Salt and pepper to taste. And taste again!

Roasted Corn: To roast the corn, remove silk from unhusked ears of corn. Smooth husks back to cover the corn. Lay on a medium-hot grill. Dip a clean burlap sack in water. Wring out slightly and place over the corn so the corn will steam. Grill 10 minutes on 1 side, turn and recover with burlap, sprinkle with water and grill another 10 minutes. A pair of gloves would be a good idea.

To roast just a few cobs at home, you can wrap the unhusked corn in foil and roast over hot coals, turning frequently, for about 20 minutes. Or you can soak the unhusked corn in water for a few minutes, then lie directly on a hot grill and roast for 15 to 20 minutes, turning several times throughout the roasting period.

Remove husks and serve with lots of butter, salt and pepper.

Carrot Cake with Cream Cheese Icing

This moist flavorful cake has become a national favorite. It can be baked in a large rectangular pan for picnics and family dinners, in round pans for an elegant layer cake, or in a bundt pan for a really special look.

4	4	eggs, beaten
1½ cups	375 mL	vegetable oil
1½ cups	375 mL	sugar
1 teaspoon	5 mL	vanilla
2 cups	500 mL	flour
1 tablespoon	15 mL	cinnamon
1 teaspoon	5 mL	baking soda
1½ teaspoons	7 mL	baking powder
1 teaspoon	5 mL	salt
3 cups	750 mL	grated carrots

Preheat oven to 350°F (180°C).

Beat eggs, add oil, sugar and vanilla and beat very well. Mix dry ingredients and stir into egg mixture. Fold in grated carrots.

Pour into greased and lightly floured pan. Cake fills 3 round layer-cake pans, a 9 x 19" (23 x 33 cm) rectangular pan or 1 bundt pan.

Bake 30 to 40 minutes for layer cakes, 50 to 60 minutes for a rectangular or bundt pan.

When cool, spread with Cream Cheese icing.

(Continued on next page.)

(Continued)

Cream Cheese Icing

4 ounces	125 g	cream cheese
½ cup	125 mL	butter
2 cups	500 mL	icing (confectioner's) sugar
1 teaspoon	5 mL	vanilla

Have both cream cheese and butter at room temperature.

Beat all ingredients until fluffy and smooth. Spread over cooled cake.

Nanaimo Bars

Nobody knows how Nanaimo, a seaside city on Vancouver Island, ever got a square named after it... but never mind. It's a delicious square and Nanaimo is proud to lend its name!

First Layer:

½ cup	125 mL	butter
4 tablespoons	60 mL	sugar
5 tablespoons	5 mL	cocoa
1	1	egg, beaten
1 teaspoon	5 mL	vanilla
2 cups	500 mL	crushed graham wafers
1 cup	250 mL	coconut
½ cup	125 mL	walnuts OR pecans

Second Layer:

3 tablespoons	45 mL	milk
2 tablespoons	30 mL	custard powder*
2 tablespoons	30 mL	butter
1 teaspoon	5 mL	vanilla
2 cups	500 mL	icing (confectioner's) sugar

Third Layer:

4	4	semisweet chocolate squares
2 tablespoons	30 mL	butter

To make first layer, melt butter in heavy saucepan or double boiler. Add sugar, cocoa and egg. Heat until slightly thickened.

Add crushed graham wafers and coconut. Chop walnuts or pecans and add. Mix and press into a 9" (23 cm) square pan. Chill.

Mix milk, custard powder, butter, vanilla and icing sugar. Spread over first layer. Chill.

Melt chocolate slowly, add butter. Spread over second layer. Chill and cut into squares.

*Note: Custard powder is available in the baking section of most stores.

A Clam Bake From Sea To Sea

It used to be that Clam Bakes were reserved for those Canadians lucky enough to live close to the ocean. However, good fish stores have changed that, and Canadians all across the country can now enjoy an old-fashioned Calm Bake.

An old custom that dates back to North American Indians, the clam bake is a wonderful excuse to be outdoors, to gather with friends and family, to celebrate friendship and food! It has become popular in the last few years to have mussels along with the clams so, in fact, the Clam Bake has now become a Clam and Mussel Feed.

MENU

● ● ● ●

Steamed Clams and Mussels
Melted Butter
Vinegar and/or Lemon Juice
Caesar Salad
A Trio of Cheese Breads
Spice Cake with Raisin Icing... page 144

Jig, Not Dance

*"Jigging was the way it was done. When we wanted fish chowder,
I dropped the jigger overboard. It was made so that when drawn
through the water it looked like a caplin. There was no need to bait
the hook. The fish jumped after what they thought was a fish and
caught on the first jig."*

Steamed Clams and Mussels

For an authentic clam and mussel feed, you should properly be on a beach somewhere – arranging a fire within rocks and stones, covering it with seaweed and then steaming the clams and mussels in wire-bottomed boxes covered with tarpaulins. However, there aren't too many Canadians who have the ocean or the tools needed for such authenticity, so try our modern version!

1 quart	1 L	soft clams and mussels, per person
¼ cup	50 mL	melted butter, per person
¼ cup	50 mL	lemon juice and vinegar, per person

Scrub clam and mussel shells with hard brush and rinse well.

Select large pot with tight-fitting cover. Place about 1" (2.5 cm) water in bottom of pot. Bring to a boil.

Throw in clams and mussels. Cover and return to a boil.

Steam just until the shells open, 5 to 8 minutes. Discard any that have not opened.

Serve on large plate with melted butter, lemon juice and vinegar in small bowls on side for dipping. Or strain broth, add a bit of lemon juice or vinegar and use that for dipping.

A New Brunswick friend uses another way of cooking her clams and mussels; place clams and mussels in large pot with small amount of water.

Cover and bring to a boil. When it boils to a froth, lift off heat until froth settles, return to heat. Do this 3 times and clams and mussels will be perfectly steamed.

Baked Potatoes

Baked potatoes are a great favorite but they're not quite as simple as they sound – mainly because there are so many ways of achieving a good baked potato!

For a beach picnic, wrap clean potatoes in several layers of heavy duty foil and bake on the coals of the bonfire, turning frequently, for about 40 to 50 minutes. Serve with butter, sour cream, grated cheese, chives, freshly ground pepper.

For a backyard barbecue, wrap clean whole potatoes in heavy foil and bake as above on the grill. Or slice the potatoes into pieces of foil; add sliced onion, celery, mushrooms, green pepper and butter. Close each package securely and bake on grill for 30 to 40 minutes. Serve each guest one package of vegetables.

Or you could use the tried and true oven method. Preheat oven to 400°F (200°C).

Clean potatoes, rub with oil or butter and bake for about 1 hour or until soft when pinched.

A skewer inserted through flesh of potato will make it bake faster. Dress up as desired. Or follow instructions for baking potatoes in the microwave, one of the greatest talents of the microwave!

Caesar Salad

Caesar salad with its pungent, piquant dressing complements any main dish that is quieter in its approach – like the clams and mussels in this section. Prepare the ingredients in advance and then put the salad together just before serving.

Croutons:

2-3 cups	500-750 mL	bread cubes
2-3 tablespoons	30-45 mL	vegetable oil
		garlic salt to taste

Dressing:

4 tablespoons	60 mL	lemon juice
¾ cup	175 mL	vegetable oil
1	1	clove garlic, crushed
1½ teaspoon	7 mL	salt
½ teaspoon	2 mL	prepared mustard
1	1	egg yolk
2-3	2-3	anchovies (optional)
1	1	head romaine lettuce
⅓ cup	75 mL	parmesan cheese

Preheat oven to 275°F (140°C).

Spread bread cubes in shallow pan and bake for 35 to 40 minutes or until cubes are completely crisp.

Place in small bowl, sprinkle with 2 to 3 tablespoons (30-45 mL) vegetable oil and garlic salt to taste. Toss to evenly coat.

In jar with tight-fitting lid, combine lemon juice, ¾ cup (175 mL) vegetable oil, crushed garlic, salt, prepared mustard and egg yolk. If you're using anchovies, mash them and add to dressing at this point. Shake well.

Wash and dry lettuce. To crisp, tie in plastic bag and refrigerate for several hours.

At serving time, tear into bite-sized pieces, place in large bowl, toss lightly with dressing. Add croutons and Parmesan cheese. Toss again.

Serves 6 to 8.

Flipper Pie

Clean flippers well, making sure to cut off all fat. Some people parboil the flippers about 20 minutes. Dredge with flour. Add seasoning and put in pan with fat back pork, onion and bacon. When nearly cooked – about 2 hours, vegetables may be added and a rich biscuit-type tipping put on. The meat should be tasty and tender when cooked. Serve with lemon wedges.

Recipe from "Labrador Cook Book"

Cheddar Cheese Bread

1	1	French bread loaf
		butter OR margarine
		mayonnaise, as required
		garlic salt OR onion salt,
		as required
2 cups	500 mL	grated Cheddar cheese

Preheat oven to 400°F (200°C).

Cut bread in half vertically, then cut each piece in half horizontally. Place under broiler, cut side up, and toast until golden.

Spread generously with butter or margarine, then with mayonnaise. Sprinkle with garlic or onion salt. Sprinkle grated Cheddar cheese evenly over entire surface.

If serving immediately, place in oven for 10 to 15 minutes. If serving later, cover with plastic wrap and refrigerate until serving time, then toast as above.

Feta Cheese Topped Bread

1	1	French bread loaf
		butter Or margarine,
		as required
		garlic salt, as required
1½ cups	375 mL	feta cheese

Preheat oven to 400°F (200°C).

Cut bread in half vertically, then cut each piece in half horizontally. Place under broiler, cut side up, and toast until golden.

Spread generously with butter or margarine. Sprinkle with garlic salt.

Crumble feta cheese and spread evenly over loaf surfaces.

If serving immediately place in oven for 10 to 15 minutes. If serving later cover with plastic wrap and refrigerate until serving time. Then toast as above.

Parmesan Cheese Bread

1	1	French bread loaf
1 cup	250 mL	butter OR margarine
½ cup	125 mL	parmesan cheese
1 teaspoon	5 mL	paprika
1	1	garlic clove *, crushed

Preheat oven to 400°F (200°C).

Cut the French loaf in half vertically, then cut each piece in half horizontally. Place under broiler, cut side up, and roast until golden.

Spread generously with butter or margarine.

Mix the Parmesan cheese, paprika and garlic. Spread over toasted bread.

If serving immediately place in oven for 10 to 15 minutes. If serving later in the day, cover with plastic wrap and refrigerate until serving time. Then toast as above.

Note: Instead of the fresh garlic, you could use ¼ teaspoon (1 mL) garlic powder.

Notes

Come for Tea, Come for Coffee

Canadian pioneers were often isolated – miles from the nearest neighbor, so visitors were always welcomed and always offered food. In fact, the first thing said after "Hello" was, "Will you stay for tea... or coffee?"

So Canadian cooks have developed a good selection of foods to have with tea and coffee – lots of quick breads and coffee cakes, cookies and steaming fresh muffins or biscuits. Generally, the more formal occasions belonged to tea – when the Ladies Aid met or the preacher came to call. Then out would come the daintier cakes and cookies, perhaps a pound cake or fruit cake. If the strawberries were ripe, it was the best of all times – Strawberry Shortcake Time!

When coffee was served, it was more likely to call for heartier fare, like lunch for the men in the fields or midmorning break on washing day. Then would the date-filled cookies be served, or fresh steaming bran muffins, or everyone's old favorite, Spice Cake.

MENU

● ● ● ●

Tea, Steeped in Tradition
Tea Biscuits
Strawberry Shortcake
Almond Shortcake
Pound Cake/Cherry Cake... page 78/79
Lemon Coconut Squares... page 24
Assortment of Canadian Tarts... pages 89, 90, 91
Coffee, Brewed and Black, Strong and Sure
Blueberry Buckle Coffee Cake... page 176
Cranberry Loaf... page 268
Trilby's, A Date-Filled Cookie
Blueberry Muffins/Bran Muffins
Spice Cake

Cream Biscuits

Tea biscuits and their many variations have long been part of Canada's life – at strawberry teas and festivals across the country, for tea at the famous Empress Hotel in Victoria, for threshers at harvest time and cowboys at branding time. Sometimes, they were round, sometimes square, often triangular... but always appreciated! When split open and served with fresh fruit and whipped cream, they became shortcakes.

1 ½ cups	375 mL	flour
3 teaspoons	15 mL	baking powder
2 tablespoons	30 mL	sugar
½ teaspoon	2 mL	salt
1 cup	250 mL	cream

Preheat oven to 425°F (210°C).

Mix dry ingredients. Quickly stir in cream. Add more, if necessary – dough should be soft, slightly sticky but manageable.

Turn out on lightly floured board. Work into smooth round. Pat or gently roll into rectangle.

Fold dough over 4 times. Pat or roll into rectangle again. (This makes biscuits flaky and easy to separate into layers). Dough should be about ½" (1.5 cm) thick.

Cut with round cookie cutter or biscuit cutter.

Place on greased baking sheet and bake for 10 minutes or until lightly browned.

Serve with strawberry jam or Canadian honey.

Yields 10 to 12 biscuits.

Strawberry Shortcake

1	1	recipe of Cream Biscuits, page 136
		Sweetened Whipped Cream, page 35
2 cups	500 mL	fresh strawberries

Prepare Cream Biscuits. Let cool. Prepare whipped cream. Slice strawberries. Leave a few berries whole to use as garnish

Split biscuits in half. Spread bottom with few sliced strawberries and a spoonful of whipped cream. Cover with top part of biscuit. Top with more whipped cream and berries.

Currant Scones

Variations of scones are to be found in historic cookbooks from every province of Canada. Some call for oatmeal, some for an egg, others for raisins and peel. Typically, they are served hot from the oven.

3 cups	750 mL	flour
2 tablespoons	30 mL	sugar
2 tablespoons	30 mL	baking powder
1 teaspoon	5 mL	salt
6 tablespoons	90 mL	butter OR margarine
1	1	egg, slightly beaten
1 ¼ cups	300 mL	cream
4 tablespoons	60 mL	currants

Preheat oven to 450°F (220°C).

Mix flour, sugar, baking powder and salt. Cut or work in butter or margarine until mixture resembles coarse crumbs.

Beat egg with cream. Wash currants and add to cream. Blend egg mixture with dry ingredients to form soft slightly sticky dough. Add more cream if necessary.

Turn dough onto lightly floured board. Shape into ball. Pat or roll into 2 circles, approximately ¾" (2 cm) thick.

Cut each circle into 8 pie shaped wedges and place on greased cookie sheet.

Bake for about 10 minutes or until lightly browned.

Makes 16 scones.

Almond Shortcake

This superb version of Christmas shortbread is baked in a round cake pan or pie plate, and then served in the round on an attractive plate.

¾ cup	175 mL	butter
1 cup	250 mL	white sugar
4 tablespoons	60 mL	almond paste
1	1	egg, beaten
½ teaspoon	2 mL	almond flavoring
2 cups	500 mL	flour
1 teaspoon	5 mL	baking powder
½ teaspoon	2 mL	salt
5	5	almonds, halved

Preheat oven to 325°F (160°C).

Cream butter, sugar and almond paste. Add half of beaten egg and almond flavoring.

Mix with flour, baking powder and salt. Add to creamed mixture. Knead lightly.

Lightly butter two 8" (22 cm) round cake pans or pie plates.

Press dough into pans, scoring edges with tines of fork. Brush remainder of egg over top.

Press almond halves to form a circle in center of each shortcake.

Bake for 25 minutes or until lightly browned.

Blueberry Muffins

Blueberries are most often used in Blueberry Muffins, wouldn't you know, but in this case, saskatoons could also be used.

½ cup	125 mL	butter OR margarine
¾ cup	175 mL	sugar
1	1	egg
2 cups	500 mL	flour
1 tablespoon	15 mL	baking powder
½ teaspoon	2 mL	salt
1 cup	250 mL	milk
1 cup	250 mL	blueberries

Preheat oven to 375°F (190°C).

Cream butter or margarine and sugar. Add egg and mix well.

Combine dry ingredients and add alternately with milk, stirring only to mix.

Fold in berries. Fill 12 greased muffin tins about ⅔ full.

Bake for 25 to 30 minutes, slightly longer if using frozen berries.

Bran Muffins

This recipe makes 40 large muffins, but if that's too many muffins at once, you can store the batter in the refrigerator for up to six weeks, using only what you need in each baking. Prepare batter at least a day ahead.

5 teaspoons	25 mL	baking soda
2 cups	500 mL	boiling water
1 cup	250 mL	vegetable oil
2 cups	500 mL	brown sugar
4	4	eggs
4 tablespoons	60 mL	molasses
1 teaspoon	5 mL	cinnamon
1 tablespoon	15 mL	salt
5 cups	1.25 L	flour
4 cups	1 L	buttermilk
5 cups	1.25 L	all bran breakfast cereal
1 cup	250 mL	chopped dates

Preheat oven to 400°F (200°C).

Add soda to boiling water and let it cool. In large bowl, beat vegetable oil, sugar and eggs well. Stir in molasses.

Mix cinnamon and salt with flour and add to creamed mixture alternately with buttermilk.

Add soda water mixture, all bran cereal and dates. Refrigerate batter at least 24 hours before using.

Fill greased muffin tins ¾ full and bake for 20 to 25 minutes or until toothpick inserted in center comes out clean.

Trilby's

This date-filled oatmeal cookie recipe comes from the personal hand-written recipe book of Mrs. Gerald Rutherford of Manitoba. A thick layer of date filling is baked between 2 layers of rolled oatmeal cookie dough. The result is a thick, hearty and absolutely delicious cookie.

		Date Filling, page 143
2 cups	500 mL	rolled oats
1 cup	250 mL	brown sugar
2 cups	500 mL	flour
2 teaspoons	10 mL	baking soda
1 teaspoon	5 mL	cream of tartar
¾ teaspoon	3 mL	salt
⅔ cup	150 mL	butter
1 cup	250 mL	sour milk*

Preheat oven to 400°F (200°C).

Prepare Date Filling first.

To make cookie, mix dry ingredients. Work in butter until mixture is crumbly. Stir in sour milk. Roll cookie dough on a well-floured board until very thin. Cut with large round cookie cutter.

Arrange circles of cookie dough on greased baking sheet. Place 1 tablespoon (15 mL) date filling in center of each circle. Cover with another circle of cookie dough, pressing edges together slightly. Continue until all cookies are filled and covered.

Bake for 10 to 12 minutes or until lightly browned. The flavor improves after storing in airtight container for several days.

Makes about 24 double cookies.

*Note: To sour milk, stir 1 tablespoon (15 mL) vinegar into 1 cup (250 mL) milk, and let stand for 5 minutes.

(Continued on next page.)

(Continued)

Date Filling:

1 cup (½ pound)	250 mL (250 g)	dates
1 cup	250 mL	water
¼ cup	50 mL	sugar

Chop dates and simmer with water until thick and mushy. Add more water if necessary. Stir in sugar. Remove from heat.

Spice Cake with Raisin Icing

This moist spice cake was a favorite for the threshers – hearty and tasty. It can be served with a Baked On Crumb Topping, below, as a quick coffee cake or a dessert – topped with whipped cream or iced with Raisin Icing.

2 cups	500 mL	flour
1 cup	250 mL	sugar
1 teaspoon	5 mL	baking soda
1½ teaspoons	7 mL	cinnamon
1 teaspoon	5 mL	nutmeg
½ teaspoon	2 mL	cloves
½ teaspoon	2 mL	salt
¾ cup	175 mL	butter or margarine
1	1	egg, beaten
1 cup	250 mL	buttermilk

Preheat oven to 350°F (180°C).

Combine dry ingredients in large bowl. With fingers on spoon, work in butter or margarine until mixture is crumbly. Mix egg and buttermilk and stir into first mixture.

Pour into greased 9" square (2.5 L) baking pan. If using Baked On Crumb Topping, below, make it at this stage and sprinkle over batter.

Bake for 40 minutes or until lightly browned. If using Raisin Icing, next page, cool cake before icing.

(Continued on next page.)

(Continued)

Raisin Icing

1½ cups	375 mL	icing (confectioner's) sugar
2 tablespoons	30 mL	soft butter
2 tablespoons	30 mL	milk
1 teaspoon	5 mL rum	flavoring or vanilla
2 tablespoons	30 mL	raisins, washed

Beat icing sugar, butter, milk and flavoring together. Chop raisins coarsely and add to mixture. Spread on cooled cake.

Baked On Crumb Topping For Coffee Cake

½ cup	125 mL	flour
¼ cup	50 mL	sugar
3 tablespoons	45 mL	butter or margarine

Work ingredients together until they form crumbs. Sprinkle over the batter before baking.

Notes

Newfoundland
Tastes of the land... and its history

As early as the year 1497, ships from Western Europe crossed the North Atlantic Ocean to fish on the Grand Banks off the coasts of Newfoundland. Fish of all kinds flourished in the shallow sunlit water – cod, capelin, halibut and sole.

In fact, the fishing was so good that when Britain claimed the territory in 1583, they had to fight French, Spanish, Dutch and pirate ships – just to keep control of the valuable fishing grounds.

Also because of the wonderful fishing grounds, settlement was slow. The British government, wanting to preserve the fishing for their summer expeditions, required that all ships' crews return home at the end of the season – except for a few "livyers" who were allowed to "live over" during the winter just to keep an eye on the place. In spite of the regulations, however, a few small scattered settlements did get established, peopled mainly by English, Irish and Scottish fishermen. Because they stayed to themselves and away from the government of the day, they retained their own languages, their own ways, an independence that still marks many Newfoundland people and areas.

However, the rules were slowly relaxed and St. John's, the administrative headquarters, became a busy center. The British Governor was pretty well in charge of things until 1855 when Newfoundland was given full colonial status with its own government and judicial system.

During World War II, the island served as an important military base and in the years following the war, Newfoundlanders began to consider the merits of joining the rest of Canada. It wasn't an easy decision for the fiercely independent citizens, but they were finally persuaded in 1949 to become Canada's tenth province.

Newfoundland's food traditions are a reflection of its history as an isolated island settled by self-reliant fisherman.

Cod is the staple and always has been. In Newfoundland, fish means codfish. Other fish are used, of course, but they are referred to by their specific names – as salmon, capelin, halibut, etc.

Cod is served fried, baked, with or without stuffing, as codfish balls or as

chowder. When salted, it is used for codfish cakes, "boiled up" with potatoes, or used in combination with brewis, a hardtack biscuit that is soaked and cooked along with the cod. Cod tongues and sounds (air sacks) are breaded and fried, and codfish heads are used to flavor soup. The homemakers in Newfoundland used their cod as thoroughly as the native women on the prairies used every possible part of the buffalo. The methods may change but the philosophy was "waste not, want not" carries throughout the country.

As fresh meats were scarce in the early days, salted beef and salted pork came to be regarded as company fare. Even today, diced salt pork is fried crisp into scrunchions and sprinkled over other dishes for flavoring. Salt pork also provided the fat for buns, cakes and chowders.

Molasses from the West Indies was cheaper than sugar and therefore used as the sweetener in all baked goods as well as the basis for "screech", the famous Newfoundland rum. As well, molasses was spread on a slice of bread to make the famous lip smacking "lassie bread". Dried fruits were used until berry-picking time, but once the wild fruits were ripe, everyone headed out for partridge berries, blueberries, raspberries, strawberries, dewberries, pineberries, squashberries and bakeapplies – a yellow berry that looks like a raspberry.

If you are blessed, a Newfoundlander may invite you to a "Scoff", a "Mug Up" or a "Boil Up in the Woods". Or you may be served a Jiggs Dinner, Seal Flipper Pie, Fried Cod Tongues, Figgidy Duff with a Molasses Coady or... best of all, to some minds... a piece of golden fried codfish embellished with crisp scrunchions.

Celebrate the foods of Newfoundland!

A Scoff from Newfoundland

A "Scoff" in Newfoundland is a big feed with good friends. In years gone by, everyone would bring something to the "Scoff", a vegetable dish or some fresh cod or perhaps a Figgidy Duff, the famous steamed pudding of Newfoundland. In fact, a "Scoff" was the forerunner of today's popular potluck dinners, another occasion when Canadians share food and fun!

Along with food, a "Scoff" includes visiting, singing, games and perhaps even a little dancing. People in isolated communities learned to make their own fun!

The following menu includes a cod recipe, of course, for cod is king. Newfoundlanders are lucky that way – they have the very best fish at their doorsteps. As well, there's a Jiggs Dinner which would likely have been served to company for it contains corned beef. Top it all off with two terrific desserts.

MENU
● ● ● ●
Cod Au Gratin
Jiggs Dinner and Pease Pudding
Figgidy Duff with Molasses Coady
Fresh Berries
Classic Fruit Cake

Cod Au Gratin

Fish in Newfoundland means cod fish. In the Maritimes every bit of the cod fish is used but for this dish you only need cod fillets so you may want to buy them already filleted.

2 pounds	1 kg	cod fillets
4 tablespoons	60 mL	butter
1	1	medium onion, diced
6 tablespoons	90 mL	flour
3 cups	750 mL	milk
2 teaspoons	10 mL	salt
½ teaspoon	2 mL	ground pepper
1 cup	250 mL	grated Cheddar cheese
		dash paprika

Preheat oven to 350°F (180°C).

Divide cod into suitable-sized portions and place in greased dish.

Prepare cream sauce by melting butter, adding onion and sautéing until tender. Stir in flour. Stir in milk and cook until smooth and thickened.

Season with salt and pepper. Pour sauce over cod. Sprinkle cheese and paprika on top of the sauce.

Bake for about 40 minutes, or until fish is thoroughly cooked and sauce is nicely browned.

Serves 6 to 8.

Jiggs Dinner

This traditional Newfoundland boiled dinner became known as "Jiggs" dinner after the comic strip character Jiggs whose favorite meal was corned beef and cabbage. Cooking the meat, split peas and vegetables together gives this dish a delicious down-home flavor.

3-4 pounds	1.5-2 kg	corned beef, unsliced
2 cups	500 mL	yellow split peas
6	6	medium potatoes
6	6	medium carrots
1	1	medium turnip
1	1	medium cabbage
		butter and pepper

Place meat in large pot.

Tie peas in cheesecloth or piece of cotton. Leave some room for expansion. Place peas in pot with meat.

Cover both with water. Cover pot and simmer for 3 hours.

About 30 to 40 minutes before serving, cut vegetables into big chunks. Add prepared vegetables, except for cabbage. After 15 minutes, add cabbage and simmer for another 15 minutes or until tender.

Serve meat and vegetables on platter. Spoon peas into bowl and mash with butter and pepper to taste.

Figgidy Duff

A Newfoundland dinner is never complete without the steamed pudding known as "Figgidy Duff" and its sauce known as "Molasses Coady". Foreign sailors always looked forward to the shores of Newfoundland – partly for the wonderful fish that could be taken but also for the Figgidy Duff that the local women served.

2 cups	500 mL	soaked bread
1 cup	250 mL	raisins
½ cup	125 mL	molasses
¼ cup	50 mL	melted butter
1 teaspoon	5 mL	baking soda
1 tablespoon	15 mL	hot water
½ cup	125 mL	flour
1 teaspoon	5 mL	ginger, allspice, cinnamon EACH
¼ teaspoon	1 mL	salt

Cut bread into cubes and soak in water for a few minutes. Gently squeeze moisture from bread and measure amount required.

Add raisins and molasses and mix with fork. Add melted butter.

Dissolve baking soda in hot water and add to mixture. Stir flour with spices and salt, then add to mixture.

Pack mixture into pudding bag or steamed pudding mold and steam approximately 2 hours. (See Plum Pudding, page 66, for steaming directions.

Serve hot with Molasses Coady.

Molasses Coady

1 cup	250 mL	molasses
¼ cup	50 mL	water
3 tablespoons	45 mL	butter
1 tablespoon	15 mL	vinegar

Put all ingredients into small heavy saucepan and simmer for 10 minutes.

Spoon over pudding.

Bake Apples

Bake apples are yellow, deliciously flavored berries, high in Vitamin C and much beloved by Newfoundlanders. In years gone by, they used to bring home hundreds of gallons of the ripe berries for making jams, tarts and other desserts.

Classic Fruit Cake

Fruit cake for Christmas is an old Canadian tradition dating back to the first settlers. One Newfoundland housewife brags that her recipe is 200 years old, "brought from Ireland by the nuns".

Beautifully decorated fruit cakes are also used at weddings, a custom dating back to the 17th century England. The bride and groom together cut the first piece of cake and then small pieces are passed to each guest. To refuse a piece of wedding cake is considered bad luck for the couple being married – so everyone must have some cake!

4 pounds	2 kg	raisins and currants
1 pound	500 g	dates, dried apricots, cherries, peel*
½ cup	125 mL	rum
2 cups	500 mL	nuts (optional)
1½ cups	375 mL	butter
2 cups	500 mL	brown sugar
8	8	eggs
1 cup	250 mL	molasses (fancy)
4½ cups	1 L	flour
1 teaspoon	5 mL	allspice, cinnamon, nutmeg, mace EACH
1 teaspoon	5 mL	salt
1 teaspoon	5 mL	baking soda
½ cup	125 mL	strong coffee OR fruit juice

Preheat oven to 275°F (140°C).

Wash raisins and currants. Drain. Add remaining dried fruit, sprinkle with rum and let stand for several hours or overnight. Add nuts, if desired.

In large bowl, cream butter and sugar. Beat in eggs 1 at a time. Stir in molasses.

Sift flour, spices, salt and baking soda. Stir into creamed mixture alternately with the coffee or fruit juice. Fold in fruit and nuts, if used.

(Continued on next page.)

(Continued)

Line Christmas cake pans or four 8 x 4" (20 x 10 cm) loaf tins with greased brown paper.

Bake for 2 to 5 hours, depending on the pan size. Bake until toothpick inserted into cake comes out clean.

*Note: Mix fruit to make a total about of 1 pound (500 g).

Suggested Baking Times for Fruit Cake:
4" (10 cm) square, 2 to 2½ hours
6" (15 cm) square, 3 to 3½ hours

Notes

Prince Edward Island
Tastes of the land, and its history

The smallest Canadian province, a beautiful island in the Gulf of St. Lawrence, was home only to Micmac Indians until France claimed it and established a small colony of settlers. Through the years, they discovered the richness of the soil of this new land and ended up growing enough potatoes, buckwheat and barley to ship extra produce to Louisbourg, the fortified French military base across the water on Cape Breton.

During the mid-1700's, these few settlers were joined by some 5,000 Acadians who fled there from Nova Scotia, hoping to escape the hostilities between France and England. When the British captured Louisbourg in 1758, these Acadians were deported as well, except for the determined few who hid out in the woods until soldiers departed.

Under British rule, the island's name was changed from the original Saint John to St. Johns and then to Prince Edward Island. The British also surveyed the land into 67 townships which were then distributed by lottery to various military and government favorites.

These new landlords were supposed to bring more settlers to the area, and pay rent to England to cover civil administration costs. The plan never worked well. Landlords generally failed to live up to the agreement and the settlers who came soon felt oppressed when they saw the freehold arrangements of other colonies. Land ownership problems lasted for over 100 years, until union with Canada in 1873. At that time, the Island government borrowed money from the Canadian government and bought out the absentee landlords.

Access was also a continual problem for Islanders, particularly in winter when ice blocked the Northumberland Strait. Thus the Islanders learned to be particularly independent, depending on their own resources for work, food and entertainment. They grew their own food and grain for whole-wheat bread, oatmeal for porridge, vegetables for the table. Cheese was made at home. Meals were home cured. Yards of sausages hung from the ceiling to dry. Oysters, clams and lobsters were hooked from under the rocks near shore. Trout, mackerel and cod were bartered for a keg of Labrador salt herring. Bannocks, scones and buckwheat pancakes were spread with molasses for a treat.

Barn raisings, land clearing, plowing, fertilizing and harvesting were

accomplished by "Frolics". Neighbors were invited, food prepared and a supply of spirits made ready. Up to 30 men came with hoes, axes, horses and wagons. Sometimes the women gathered for a "Hooking and Spinning Bee" at the same time. When the task was finished and supper dishes washed, fiddlers gathered in the barns and played old-time reels in the flickering light of lanterns.

Social life also involved harness racing, skating, hockey, curling, cross-country skiing, and the picnics and gatherings that surrounded these events.

Island cuisine reflects the intermingling of the original peoples and the English, Scots, Irish and Micmac Indians. Steamed puddings, fruit cakes, meat pies, scones, bannock, soda bread, oatmeal, buckwheat, smoked eel and a large variety of seafood are historic foods that still turn up on Prince Edward Island tables, not to mention tables all across the country, since good food has a way of traveling!

However, the 'Big Three' in Prince Edward Island are the potato, the Malpeque oyster and lobster. Potatoes grown on the rich red soil of P.E.I. are considered among the finest in the world. Malpeque oysters don't grow on the rich red soil, but the sea surrounding the Island gives them something special that sets them apart. And the lobster. What can we say about lobsters other than they are wonderful. They are a specialty in all of the Atlantic Provinces but somehow, Prince Edward Island has gotten the jump on claiming them as their own. Lobster suppers are held in community halls throughout the tourist season and many a tourist from around the world has gone home remembering the Lobster Supper in Prince Edward Island above everything else!

Celebrate the foods of Prince Edward Island!

Fresh Oysters

Oysters (enjoyed even before the Europeans arrived) are still regarded as a festive treat whether served as a stew, casserole or cold, fresh and raw - our preference for New Years!

Bring an oyster opener with you. It's a sturdy tool that will quickly shuck the meanest oyster. Keep unopened oysters cold on a bed of ice. Let everyone open their own. For accompaniment, all that is needed is sliced lemon and a pepper grinder.

Prince Edward Island
Lobster Supper

In his book, "Don't Let Them Smell the Lobsters Cooking", Stuart Trueman recalled the days when lobster was a lowly and plentiful food. "You could tell who the poor kids were by the lunches they brought to school; they ate lobster sandwiches every day."

Nowadays, the sweet-tasting lobsters from the cold Maritime waters are prized across Canada, and Prince Edward Island has captured the title of "Lobster Capital of Canada" – even though lobsters are enjoyed in other parts of the country!

What Prince Edward Island has done is to offer Lobster Suppers for Tourists – served up by community groups in community centers with a nice community feeling. It's an unbeatable combination – lobster and friendship! Charlottetown uses it in its annual "Old-Home Week", so does Summerside with its summer "Lobster Carnival", so does most every other community, sometime through the year.

A lobster supper is generally just that – lobster with lots of melted butter on the side. But there are cooks who like to serve more and occasions when more seems right... which is when fresh breads and biscuits, crisp garden vegetables, too-good-to-resist desserts appear along with the lobster. The Mighty Lobster!

MENU
● ● ● ●

Lobster in the Shell
Melted Butter
Picnic Potato Salad... page 12
Garden Vegetable Platter
Sour Cream Dressing
Currant Scones... page 138
Lemon Meringue Pie

Lobster in the Shell

Lobsters are a sight for sore eyes – with their white juicy flesh enclosed in bright red shells. But more than that, of course, they are a taste treat.

1-1½ pounds   500-750 g   lobster, per person
                                        a big pot, lots of boiling
                                        water and salt

Fill a large kettle with enough water to cover the lobsters you wish to boil. To each quart (1 L) of water, add 1 tablespoon (15 mL) salt.

When water is boiling, grasp each lobster by the back, plunge it into water head first, pushing lobster underwater.

Boil for 15 to 20 minutes, then remove at once.

Place lobster on their backs and with a sharp knife slit across under-part of each lobster.

Remove black vein and discard all organs near head section except the red roe in the females and the brownish green liver. Crack claws.

Serve with individual pots of melted butter, wedges of lemon and lots of large napkins!

Garden Vegetable Platter

Select and prepare fresh vegetables: cucumber slices, ripe red tomato wedges, green pepper strips, fresh young radishes, cauliflower florets, snow peas, mushrooms, tiny broccoli spears, green beans – lightly cooked, slivered carrots, celery stocks. Arrange on a platter or tray and serve with the following dressing.

Sour Cream Dressing

1 cup	250 mL	sour cream
1 tablespoon	15 mL	vinegar
1 teaspoon	5 mL	sugar
½ teaspoon	2 mL	salt

Combine ingredients and stir well.

Lemon Meringue Pie

Early Canadians expected great things of their lemon pies. Here is what writer Margaret Galloway said, "We have lemon pie and if you ever taste another quite as delicious, you are luckier than I. Filling soft, yet firm enough to stand up when cut, clear with little flecks of rind in it, no sparing of butter and lemons, and overall a deep snowdrift of meringue, the uneven swoops of it pale gold".

1	1	baked pie shell in 9" (23 cm) pie plate
1 cup	250 mL	sugar
6 tablespoons	90 mL	cornstarch
¼ teaspoon	1 mL	salt
½ cup	125 mL	cold water
2 cups	500 mL	boiling water
4	4	egg yolks, beaten
3 tablespoons	45 mL	butter
½ cup	125 mL	lemon juice
1 teaspoon	5 mL	lemon rind

Meringue:

4	4	egg whites
¼ teaspoon	1 mL	cream of tartar
6 tablespoons	90 mL	sugar

Prepare pie shell recipe, page 165. Bake until lightly browned.

Preheat oven to 350°F (180°C).

In heavy saucepan or double boiler, mix sugar, cornstarch and salt with cold water. Make sure all lumps are worked out. Gradually add boiling water and cook until thickened, stirring constantly.

Beat egg yolks slightly, stir some of hot mixture into the egg yolks, then return everything to saucepan and cook for 3 minutes, stirring constantly.

(Continued on next page.)

(Continued)

Remove from heat; add butter, lemon juice and rind. Cool and pour into bake shell.

For meringue, beat egg whites and cream of tartar until frothy.

Add sugar slowly while beating, until whites stand in peaks. Pile on top of lemon filling, drawing meringue right out to edges.

Bake for 15 to 20 minutes or until top is golden brown. Cool at room temperature to prevent drops of moisture forming on top. (Or use the following recipe for foolproof meringue.)

Foolproof Meringue

This is well worth the extra effort. It's creamy and light and guaranteed to hold its tears!

1 tablespoon	15 mL	cornstarch
2 tablespoons	30 mL	cold water
½ cup	125 mL	boiling water
4	4	egg whites*
½ teaspoon	2 mL	cream of tartar
		pinch of salt
½ cup	125 mL	sugar

Preheat oven to 350°F (180°C).

In small saucepan, blend cornstarch and cold water. Add boiling water and stir well. Cook, stirring constantly, until thickened.

Remove from heat, cover with plastic wrap and cool to room temperature.

Place egg whites, cream of tartar and salt in straight-sided small mixing bowl. Beat to soft peak state. Continue to beat while gradually adding sugar until mixture is stiff and sugar is completely dissolved.

Turn mixer to low speed and gradually beat in cornstarch mixture. Beat briefly at high speed.

Spread over pie filling, carefully sealing meringue to pastry edges to prevent shrinking.

Bake for about 15 minutes or until golden.

*Note: Have the egg whites at room temperature.

Frozen No-Fail Pastry

This recipe can be prepared ahead of time, divided into 5 portions and
frozen. Then, you may thaw and use the dough whenever needed.
This pastry may be rolled and reworked without any loss of its
tenderness or taste. It will make enough pastry for 5, 2–crust pies.

6 cups	1.5 L	flour
1 teaspoon	5mL	baking powder
1 tablespoon	15 mL	brown sugar
2 teaspoon	10 mL	salt
1 pound	454 g	lard
½ cup	125 mL	butter
1	1	egg, beaten
1 teaspoon	15 mL	vinegar
¼ cup	175 mL	water

In large bowl, mix flour, baking powder, sugar and salt. Cream lard
and butter. Add egg, vinegar and water. Cream well and stir in dry
ingredients.

Flour hands and bread board. Work dough until smooth and shape in
small loaf. Divide in 5 equal portions and freeze until needed.

Notes

Nova Scotia
Tastes of the land... and its history

For centuries, Nova Scotia was home only to native Indians. A few fishermen came from Europe, a few navigators looking for China, but other than that, Nova Scotia was pretty much left to its own.

However, once settlement began, it began with a vengeance... literally! France established colonies in North America in the 1600's but life was never very stable. Military forces from New England states raided them, and because of various European wars, the colony of Nova Scotia, then known as Acadia, passed from French control to English and back again.

Under the terms of the Treaty of Utrecht, in 1713, France kept Ile Royale (Cape Breton) while the rest of the territory was ceded to Britain. It was then that France built mighty Louisbourg, a fortified military base with a permanent garrison, a lively town that housed 4,000 people by 1750.

The threat posed by this prosperous and well-fortified town finally convinced Britain to get serious about her Nova Scotia holdings. Enticing offers of free passage, free land and a year's free provisions brought 2,500 people (mostly ex-soldiers) who wanted to relocate in this new land. Unfortunately, the first winter was very hard on the new arrivals – up to one-third died of starvation, poor living conditions and typhus – but those who remained went on to build the beginnings of Halifax.

At this stage, Halifax was very much a garrison town – very British, very social. One of the many events at Government House was written up in the Royal Gazette, "On Thursday evening last the Governor and Mrs. Wentworth gave a ball and supper to the ladies and gentlemen of the Town and the Officers of the Army and Navy which was altogether the most brilliant and successful entertainment ever given in the country".

Inns and coffee houses advertised "hot mutton pies, beef soup and mutton broth."[1] There were strawberries and cream and Sillabub (a creamy dessert), pickled herring and bear-hams.

Social life for the elite included picnics and chowder parties, skating parties, sleigh rides, balls and leves. For the poor, life was not so easy; it was molasses, salt cod and hard work.

Meanwhile, incidents and skirmishes still flared up between French and British military forces. The Acadian settlers were in a vulnerable position with both French and English expecting their support. When asked to swear an oath of loyalty to the British crown, most refused. Consequently, in 1755, the British commander ordered them deported. Just like that, over 13,000 people were loaded onto ships and sent to exile – either back to European lands or to friendly American territories.

In turn, the British invited New England settlers to join the colony and take over lands previously owned by the Acadians. Some 4,500 accepted the invitation. Other settlers came from the British Isles.

Soon after this, the mighty Louisbourg was captured, bringing all of Nova Scotia under British control.

However, before the province had a chance to breathe a sigh of relief, the American colonies to the south rebelled against England and in the Declaration of Independence signaled their complete breakaway from England's control. The war that followed divided families and neighbors. American citizens who showed a loyalty to Britain feared for their lives; some were even tarred, feathered and driven away. Houses were sacked, properties confiscated and civil rights denied. Such persecution continued even when the war was over… so much so that the Loyalists, as they were known, had to flee for their lives.

Thirty thousand came to Nova Scotia, more people than the province had ever seen, and the effect was profound. New England customs and food were introduced: corn husking bees, quilting parties, a love for seafood, fried oysters, steamed clams and lobsters.

Historian Helen Creighton said of the settlers: "Where food is concerned, people were prudent and stocked their houses the way they stocked their ships, in great quantities with salt beans put down in brine, and cucumbers, sauerkraut, salt fish, salt pork, puddings and sausages".

By the same token, some new settlers were so poor that for months on end they had nothing to eat but dried fish and potatoes. An old ditty recalls, "herrin' and taters, the food of the land; if you don't like it, you can starve and be dammed".[2]

Thus did a province grow… ending up with an interesting political past and a delicious food present.

Celebrate the food of Nova Scotia!

Nova Scotia Chowder Party

Celebrate Nova Scotia's colorful sea history with a Chowder Party…
a great way to celebrate any number of occasions… Christmas Eve,
after-theatre, supper-at-home, or a special party outdoors – preferably
on the beach.

The chowder can be made ahead and reheated but there should be lots
of it and at least two varieties. Chowder is substantial enough to be
a meal in itself but it is served as a soup in a soup plate. Keep hot in
an heirloom soup tureen, chafing dish, bean pot, casserole dish or…
keep hot in a soup pot and invite guests to help themselves. Chowders
can be as formal or informal as you make them. They are amazingly
obliging.

Be sure to serve with an assortment of fresh breads and crackers
– especially the hard round hollow crackers that are called "oyster"
crackers.

You may wish to add a crisp green salad. And, of course, top off the
party with one of Nova Scotia's special desserts – wedges of Blueberry
Pie, squares of Hot Gingerbread with dollops of whipped cream, or
Cranberry Crisp with thick cream.

MENU
● ● ● ●
Atlantic Fish Chowder
Clam Chowder
Corn Chowder Bisque
Oyster Crackers
Bread Sticks
Oyster Crackers
Bread Sticks
Green Salad with Lemon Mustard Dressing
Blueberry Pie
Hot Gingerbread with Sweetened Whipped Cream
Cranberry Crisp… page 186 OR
Blueberry Buckle

Atlantic Fish Chowder

Cooks at sea had a reputation for excellence and ingenuity, in spite of their difficult working conditions. From the limited supplies of canned milk, salt pork, potatoes, flour and hard biscuits, they concocted wonderful Maritime chowders... featuring the catch of the day.

1½ pounds	750 g	fish fillets*
½ pound	250 g	shrimp, scallops (optional)
4 ounces	125 g	salt pork*
1	1	onion, chopped
¾ cup	175 mL	chopped celery
2 tablespoons	30 mL	flour
1	1	chicken bouillon cube
2 cups	500 mL	water
2 cups	500 mL	diced potatoes
		salt and pepper to taste
2 cups	500 mL	milk*

Cut fish fillets into large chunks. Prepare shrimp and scallops, if using. Set aside.

Dice salt pork or bacon and fry in saucepan until crisp and brown. Remove and set aside.

Add onion and celery to remaining fat and sauté until tender, about 5 minutes. Stir in flour.

Dissolve bouillon cube in water and add to onion mixture. Add potato, salt and pepper. Simmer until potatoes are almost tender, about 10 minutes.

Add fish fillets, shrimp and scallops. Simmer for 10 minutes or until fish is flaky. Add milk. Heat for a few minutes.

Serve with the crispy salt pork or crumbled bacon.

Serves 6 to 8.

*Notes: Fish fillets can be cod, haddock, halibut or other white fish. Instead of salt pork, you could use 2 slices of bacon. For the milk, you could use diluted canned milk – it works very well for chowders.

Clam Chowder

This recipe calls for canned baby clams. However, if you're fortunate enough to live by the ocean or near a good fish store, you can get the real thing.

10 ounces	284 mL	canned baby clams
1½ cups	375 mL	chicken broth*
1½ teaspoons	7 mL	thyme
1½ teaspoons	7 mL	paprika
1 teaspoon	5 mL	pepper
3	3	large potatoes
6	6	bacon slices, diced
3	3	medium onions
1½ tablespoons	25 mL	flour
¾ teaspoon	3 mL	curry powder
½ cup	125 mL	dry white wine
3-4 cups	750 mL-1 L	milk

Drain liquor from clams into saucepan and save clams for later.

Add chicken broth, thyme, paprika and pepper. Cube potatoes and add as well. Simmer for 15 minutes.

Sauté bacon until slightly brown. Remove and add to potato mixture.

Chop onions and sauté in remaining bacon fat. Sprinkle flour and curry powder over onions, stir and cook for a few minutes. Add to potato mixture, stirring well. Add wine. Simmer until potatoes are soft.

Add reserved clams and milk. Heat gently.

Serves 6 to 8.

*Note: Chicken broth may be made with 1 chicken bouillon cube dissolved in 1½ cups (375 mL) water.

Corn Chowder Bisque

Corn chowder – thick and steaming – is wonderful for hearty appetites and happy times.

4	4	bacon slices
1	1	medium onion, chopped
2 tablespoons	30 mL	flour
2 cups	500 mL	diced potato
2 x 14 ounce	2 x 398 mL	creamed corn (2 cans)
10 ounces	284 mL	tomato soup* (1 can)
2 cups	500 mL	water
2	2	chicken bouillon cubes
1 teaspoon	5 mL	salt
¼ teaspoon	1 mL	pepper
		fresh parsley, finely chopped

Fry bacon until crisp. Remove and set aside.

Sauté onion in remaining bacon fat. Stir in flour. Remove and set aside. Add potato, corn, tomato soup, water, chicken cubes and reserved bacon. Simmer 15 minutes or until potato is tender.

Add salt and pepper. Heat thoroughly.

To serve, sprinkle chopped parsley over top.

Serves 6.

*Note: In place of tomato soup, 1 cup (250 mL) canned tomatoes could be used.

Green Salad with Lemon Mustard Dressing

This is a terrific combination of romaine lettuce and marinated mushrooms. Serve it as a texture and taste contrast to soup, as this menu suggests, or serve it whenever you want a good lettuce salad.

¼ cup	50 mL	lemon juice
⅔ cup	150 mL	vegetable oil
2 tablespoons	30 mL	brown sugar
1½ teaspoons	7 mL	salt
1 teaspoon	5 mL	dry mustard
½ teaspoon	2 mL	freshly ground pepper
½ pound	250 g	mushrooms, sliced
4	4	green onions, chopped
1	1	large romaine lettuce

Combine lemon juice, oil, sugar, salt, dry mustard and pepper. Mix until thick and blended. Add mushrooms and green onions. Let marinate for 2 to 3 hours.

Wash and dry lettuce well ahead of time so that it will be crisp at serving time. Tear into bite-sized pieces. Just before serving, toss with dressing.

Serves 8.

Hot Gingerbread

A Maritime author, Helen Wilson, fondly recalled her mother's Gingerbread. Licking the mixing bowl was the best part, "We'd scrape out the last remains of the heady gingerbread mixture".[3]

½ cup	125 mL	butter OR lard
½ cup	124 mL	sugar
2	2	eggs
1 cup	250 mL	molasses
2¼ cups	550 mL	flour
1 teaspoon	5 mL	ginger
1 teaspoon	5 mL	cinnamon
½ teaspoon	2 mL	salt
2 teaspoons	20 mL	baking soda
1 cup	250 mL	boiling water

Preheat oven to 350°F (180°C).

Cream butter or lard with sugar. Add eggs and bet well. Add molasses and stir. Mix flour, ginger, cinnamon and salt. Add to creamed mixture and stir well.

Dissolve baking soda in boiling water and stir into first mixture. The batter will be thin – do not add extra flour.

Pour into greased 9 x 13" (23 x 33 cm) cake pan.

Bake for 35 minutes or until cake tests done.

Serve hot or cold with whipped cream or fruit.

Blueberry Pie

There are dozens of recipes using blueberries: Blueberry Grunt,
Blueberry Slump, Blueberry Buckle and Blueberry Crisp – not to
mention all the other wonderful recipes with more mundane names!
This is a wonderful recipe for Blueberry Pie, the good old-fashioned
kind that doesn't fool around – just puts pastry around blueberries and
lives happily every after!

		pastry for a 2-crust 9" (23 cm) pie shell
4 cups	1 L	fresh OR frozen blueberries
¾ cup	175 mL	sugar
3 tablespoons	45 mL	flour
½ teaspoon	2 mL	salt
1 tablespoon	15 mL	lemon juice

Preheat oven to 400°F (200°C).

Prepare pastry recipe, page 165. Line bottom of pie plate.

Wash and drain berries.

Mix sugar, flour and salt. Toss with blueberries and spread in
unbaked pie shell. Sprinkle with lemon juice. Cover with pastry. Slit
top pastry in a few places for steam to escape.

Bake for 35 to 40 minutes until pastry is browned and berries soft. If
using frozen berries, bake about 15 minutes longer.

Serve with Homemade Ice Cream, page 15 or with Sweetened
Whipped Cream, page 35.

Blueberry Buckle

This Blueberry Buckle is in fact a coffee cake with a unusual name! It's most delicious served warm with hot coffee, on a cold morning, when the rain is pouring down, in other words, whenever you need a lift and a great taste!

¾ cup	175mL	sugar
½ cup	125 mL	shortening
1	1	egg
2 cups	500 mL	flour
½ teaspoon	12 mL	salt
½ cup	2 mL	milk
2 cups	500 mL	blueberries*

Topping:

½ cup	125 mL	sugar
½ cup	125 mL	flour
½ teaspoon	2 mL	cinnamon
¼ cup	50 mL	Butter

*Note: if using frozen blueberries, rinse to remove the ice crystals. Spread on paper towel and pat dry.

Cream sugar and shortening, add egg and cream well. Stir in flour, baking powder and salt, add alternately with milk to the creamed mixture. Fold in blueberries and spread in 9" (23 cm) square pan.

Topping:

Mix sugar, flour and cinnamon. Rub in butter until mixture resembles crumbs. Sprinkle over base. Bake at 350° (180°C) for 45 to 50 minutes.

Dulse

In Atlantic Canada you'll see people happily chewing on dried reddish brown seaweed much the way they would on gum or candy. The seaweed is dulse, most of it from Grand Manaan where it is gathered and spread on the rock to dry. As well as being considered tasty to eat, it is said to have nutritional and laxative benefits.

New Brunswick
Tastes of the land... and its history

The first settlers who came to the North American territory now known as New Brunswick were of French origin, eventually to be known as Acadians. They fished the rich fishing grounds, traded with the Indians and slowly moved in on the land, discovering it to be rich and versatile as well. In one area, the French settlers drained marshes on the Chignecto peninsula and planted grains, vegetables and fruit trees.

As the settlers worked the land, around them French fought French for control of the fur and fishing trade, and French fought English for control of North America. The Acadians were caught geographically and politically between the two, unappreciated by the French and misunderstood by the English. Neither accepted the Acadians' desire for neutrality.

The treaty of Utrecht in 1713 recognized Acadia as British territory and as a result, the Acadians were required to swear an oath of allegiance to the British Crown. Like their compatriots in the Nova Scotia area, they refused and were expelled. Thus between 1755 and 1763 some ten thousand men, women and children were deported. In the confusion, families were cruelly separated, buildings were burned, crops destroyed. Only a few escaped to hide in the woods and eke out a living.

After the Treaty of Paris was signed in 1763 between England and France, Acadians were once again allowed to legally own land. Alas, during their enforced absence, new settlers from the New England states had taken over their farms and property so that most of the Acadians who came back had to start all over again. Still, they persevered and today make up 37% of the population of New Brunswick.

The next major impact to New Brunswick history came as a result of the American War of Independence. At total of 14,000 people loyal to the British cause, the loyalists, landed at the mouth of the St. John River, to make their homes in a region inhabited by only 3,000 people. Although the St. John River valley is wide and fertile; the new land was nevertheless a wilderness, with forests that had to be cleared and soil that had to be wrested from the trees.

At this time, New Brunswick was part of the entire territory controlled by the British colonial office in Halifax but the newly expanded population asked for its own colonial status and government – and got it. New Brunswick was created

in 1784, with Fredericton as the capital city.

By 1840, Saint John was a thriving city, a ship-building center, thanks to the rich timber lands in the interior. Prosperity was reflected in a glittering social life – picnics, excursions on the river, soires, parlor concerts and grand balls.

The Carleton Sentinel reported the following about an Episcopal Tea Soire held July 25, 1863. "Here the tables were spread in ample profusion and the daintiest fare – this is no exaggeration. Cakes in pyramids and every other form, and such cream which, great by itself, yet became magnificent when cunningly compounded with a quantum sufficient of sugar; and then the bread and butter, and ham, and pickles, with the tea and coffee – each the very best of its kind – all went to make up a repast tempting in the extreme."

New Brunswick was one of the founding provinces when Canada was created in 1867.

The food of New Brunswick reflects its past… of course. The native Indian tribes, Micmac and Maliseet, introduced the colonists to foods from the ocean, and to pumpkin, corn, fiddlehead ferns and other spring greens, and to the sweet sap from the maple trees that grew so will in the region.

Early Acadians made good use of wild game, chicken, pork, fish and potatoes in such dishes as: Fricot made with chicken, fish or rabbit, Pâté la Viande, Acadian Tourtière, Boiled Cod and Mackerel Dinners, Rape Pie and apple desserts such as Poutines Trou.

When the Loyalists came along, they added their original English and newer New England food traditions: Fish Chowders, Pumpkin or Squash Pie, Plum and Carrot Pudding, local fruits adapted to desserts such as Blueberry Buckle, Cranberry Pie and Apple Dumplings.

The resulting blend left New Brunswick with an interesting, unique and very tasty food heritage.

Celebrate the foods of New Brunswick!

New Brunswick Date with History

New Brunswick's history comes alive in two historic villages: Kings Landing Historical Settlement near Fredericton which recognizes the contributions of the Loyalists to the settlement of the province, and Village Historique d'Acadian which preserves and propagates the cultural heritage of the Acadians.

The menu for a New Brunswick meal celebrates these two dominate cultures... which means we've featured a chicken dish. Chicken simmered in its own broth is universal, but the Acadians called their version Chicken Fricot while the Loyalists called theirs Chicken Stew. The version presented here is called Chicken with Doughboys, or Chicken With Dumplings, thus avoiding any apparent show of favoritism! We've also included a Chicken Pie, a delicious old favorite with a modern presentation.

Any New Brunswick meal must include fiddleheads, the strange-looking curly frond that grows in the Maritime provinces. Years ago, home-makers had to don their rubber boots to find these elusive little greens, but nowadays, all you have to do is brave the nearest supermarket where they are available fresh in the spring, frozen all year round. Top off the New Brunswick menu with a Blueberry Crisp, a wonderful way of using the tiny blueberries that grow in so many parts of Canada.

MENU

● ● ● ●

Chicken Pie
Chicken with Dumplings
Cranberry Chutney... page 65
Squash with Maple Syrup
Fiddleheads
Cornbread or Cornmeal Muffins... page 118
Blueberry Crisp OR
Apple Crisp Or
Cranberry Crisp

Chicken Pie

You can use canned chicken in this recipe, fresh cooked chicken or leftover turkey. Whatever is used, the combination is a treat, definitely fit for company.

		pastry for a 2-crust pie, page 165
4 cups	1 L	cooked chicken
2	2	medium onions, chopped
3 tablespoons	45 mL	butter
½ pound	250 g	pork sausage meat*
½ cup	125 mL	flour
2 cups	500 mL	chicken broth*
2 cups	500 mL	milk
2 teaspoons	10 mL	salt
		pepper to taste
½ teaspoon	2 mL	thyme and sage EACH
1 cup	250 mL	sliced mushrooms

Preheat oven to 375°F (190°C).

Line the bottom of a 3-quart (3 L) casserole with pastry. Arrange cooked meat on bottom.

Sauté onion in butter, add sausage meat or bacon and fry until lightly brown. Remove onions and meat and spread over chicken or turkey.

Stir flour into remaining fat in pan. Add chicken broth and milk and cook, stirring constantly, until thick.

Add seasonings and pour sauce over meats. Sprinkle sliced mushrooms on top.

Roll out top pastry, cut some slits for steam to escape, and place over meat mixture.

(Continued on next page.)

(Continued)

Bake for about 60 minutes or until bubbling and lightly browned.

Serves 8.

Notes: In place of sausage meat, you could substitute 4 slices bacon. If you don't have chicken broth, you could use canned chicken broth or 2 chicken bouillon cubes dissolved in 2 cups (500 mL) hot water.

Fiddleheads

Fiddleheads are so named because when they emerge in the spring, their heads are tightly curled resembling the head of a violin or fiddle. The easiest way to pick fiddleheads is to visit your nearest supermarket... in which case, just follow the instructions on the package.

If you have fresh fiddleheads, wash under running water until all brown sheaves have been removed. Place in saucepan with about 1 cup (250 mL) water, cover and simmer for about 10 minutes or until stalks are just tender. Combine 1 tablespoon (15 mL) each of melted butter and lemon juice and dribble over top.

Season with salt and pepper.

Chicken with Doughboys

Chicken simmered in its own broth is one of the most flavorful of dishes, especially when it's teamed up with doughboys – otherwise known as dumplings!

1	1	frying chicken, cut up
4 cups	1 L	water
1½ teaspoon	7 mL	salt
1	1	carrot, diced
1	1	onion, chopped
1¾ cups	425 mL	flour
4 teaspoons	20 mL	baking powder
1 teaspoon	5 mL	salt
1 tablespoon	15 mL	dried parsley
1 cup	250 mL	milk

Simmer chicken, water, salt, carrot and onion in large pot for 1 ¼ hours or until chicken is tender. Remove skin and bones from chicken and return meat to broth.

To make doughboys, stir together flour, baking powder, salt and parsley. Add milk all at once and stir only to mix.

Drop by spoonful into steaming chicken broth.

Cover tightly and cook for 20 minutes without peeking.

Serves 4 to 6.

Squash with Maple Syrup

For everyday, steamed squash is very good served with butter, salt and pepper. But for special meals, it dresses up very nicely with maple syrup and spices to make a casserole dish that can be made in advance and enjoyed on the spot!

6 cups	1.5 L	cooked squash
4 tablespoons	60 mL	butter
4 tablespoons	60 mL	maple syrup
¼ teaspoon	1 mL	cinnamon
¼ teaspoon	1 mL	nutmeg
1 teaspoon	5 mL	salt
		dash freshly ground pepper

Peel squash, remove seeds, cut into pieces and steam over small amount of boiling water until soft – about 10 to 15 minutes. Drain completely and mash well.

Add remaining ingredients and whip with spoon until smooth

If serving immediately, just spoon into serving dish and dig in. If serving later, spoon into greased casserole dish and reheat later.

Serves 8.

Blueberry, Apple and Cranberry Crisps are all Canadian favorites. A fruit crisp is just what it says – a layer of fruit topped by a layer of crispy sweetness.

Blueberry Crisp

5 cups	1.25 L	fresh OR frozen blueberries
2 tablespoons	30 mL	sugar
2 tablespoons	30 mL	flour
2 tablespoons	30 mL	lemon juice

Crisp Topping:

2 cups	500 mL	brown sugar
1 cup	250 mL	butter
1⅓ cups	325 mL	flour
1 teaspoon	5 mL	cinnamon

Preheat oven to 375°F (190°C).

Spread blueberries in a 9" (23 cm) square pan. Combine 2 tablespoons (30 mL) sugar and 2 tablespoons (30 mL) flour. Sprinkle over fruit. Sprinkle lemon juice over top as well.

To make topping: With fingers, work together brown sugar, butter, flour and cinnamon until mixture is in crumbs. Sprinkle over fruit base.

Bake for 30 to 40 minutes until golden brown and bubbling.

Serve warm or cold with Sweetened Whipped Cream, page 35, or Ice Cream, page 15.

Serves 8 to 10.

Note: If using frozen berries, either thaw before assembling or increase baking time to about 60 minutes or until fruit is tender.

(Continued on next page.)

Apple Crisp

8 cups	2 L	chopped apples
4 tablespoons	60 mL	sugar
2 teaspoons	10 mL	cinnamon
4 tablespoons	60 mL	water

Cranberry Crisp

Make as Blueberry Crisp, page 185. Increase sugar to 1¼ cups (325 mL). Either fresh or frozen cranberries can be used. If using frozen, increase baking time to about 60 minutes or until fruit it tender.

Québec
Tastes of the land... and its history

New France began as a copy of Old France but it didn't take long before Canadian history and geography gave it its own character and style. The area was claimed for France by Jacques Cartier; the first colony was established by Samuel de Champlain in 1608 at "Kebec" where St. Lawrence river narrows.

The French government offered free passage and land to prospective immigrants. Land was distributed under the old feudal system of tenure with large grants or seigneuries given to soldiers and important people. Those receiving the land were required to swear loyalty to the King of France, to build a manor house, a church and a mill, and to divide their seigneuries into long narrow plots to be farmed by the colonists or habitants for a nominal fee.

The colonists in turn had to clear the land, put up stockades and buildings, plant corn, oats, barley, peas and lentils... and keep an eye out for enemy attack. It was no mean task being a pioneer!

And speaking of mean tasks, the colony needed women if it were to survive, so French authorities offered free passage, clothes and a dowry to young French women who were religious, decent and willing to risk the rigours of a new country. Nearly 1,000 "King's Girls" took up the offer and sailed for New France. Many founded large families – indeed were encouraged to do so by the award of a yearly grant of 300 livres for ten children, 400 livres for 12 or more.

During the first years, there were many shortages – milk, bread and salt among them. The new homemakers had to learn how to use what was plentiful – caribou, deer, porcupine, hares, birds and fish. Smoked or salted eel became a favorite.

As soon as possible, pigs were established so that ham, salt pork, bacon, headcheese, cretons and pickled pigs feet became standbys in Québec kitchens. Corn also became a dietary mainstay with the settlers. Easy to grow and store, it was eaten either roasted over the coals, or mashed with game or fish, or ground and used in pea soups and pancakes.

The settlers also adopted the Indian method of tapping maple trees and boiling the sap to make syrup and sugar.

Wild strawberries, raspberries, plums, cranberries, blackberries, and blueberries

were all put to use; a favorite dish was the three-crushed blueberry pie known as Cipâte aux Bleuets.

Soup was a standby, sometimes even served for breakfast. Stews, ragouts and other dishes that could be cooked in one large black iron pot were economical and easy to prepare for a large family. Pies or Tourtieres made from wild game or domestic meat were also fashionable.

In fact, the Québec homemaker managed to turn out very good meals in spite of the shortages and adjustments that had to be made. One observer traveling through the area in 1684 notes, "the excellence of the tables and the warmth of the hospitality".[1]

In the towns, officials brought over the latest in elegant French fashions, customs and foods. In a typical middle and upper-class home, according to a traveler of that time, "the meal begins with soup, together with a large helping of bread, and this is followed by every kind of fresh meat, boiled and roasted, by game, fowls, fricasseed or stewed in casseroles, all served with various sorts of salads."[2]

"...After dinner there is dessert which comprises a variety of fruit, walnuts from France or Canada, either fresh or preserved, almonds, grapes, hazelnuts, various species of berries which ripen in summer, sweet jams made up of strawberries, raspberries, blackberries and other briar fruits. Cheese also appears with the dessert, as well as milk which is taken at the end of the meal with sugar."[3]

But even while things were settling down on the home front, the political front was heating up. France and Britain ended up at war, the winner to take all the Canadian territories then under settlement. The French colonists did their part to help the French forces but it wasn't enough; Québec City fell to British troops in 1759, Montreal the following year.

French officials, soldiers and most of the wealthy class returned to France, leaving the habitants behind, their crops destroyed, animals killed, many of their sons dead. Immigration from France stopped. It was sink or swim for the French colonists still in the new world, and the fact that they survived and prospered is testimony to their strength and determination. Their province became one of the founding members of Confederation in 1867.

Celebrate the foods of Québec!

Québec Réveillon

Québec is Canada's predominantly French province, explored and settled by people from France. Even after Britain won the wars and gained control of British North America, Québec kept its French heritage, enjoying a culture, foods and history quite different from the rest of the country.

Most Québecois were Roman Catholic and religion was a very important part of everyday life... which is why many celebrations in Québec have religious roots. One of the loveliest traditions is Réveillon, a warm gathering of family and friends following the Christmas Eve midnight mass.

It was and still is an exciting time, especially for the children. For once they willingly nap early in the evening so they can go to mass and stay up past midnight to enjoy gifts, visiting and festive foods.

Our Réveillon menu includes the best of the past – the classic Tourtière – a perfect enhancement for Fruit Chili, Tarte au Sucre, the most wonderful of Canadian pies, and the crowning glory – a Bûche de Noël... so beautiful that it seems a shame to eat it.

MENU

● ● ● ●

Cretons, a Pork Pâté
The Best Crusty French Bread
Tourtière
Catsup Rouge aux Fruits, a Fruit Chili
Beet Pickles... page 57
Salade de Choux a l'Ancienne or Creamy Coleslaw
Bûche de Noël
Tarte au Sucre, a Sweet Pie

Cretons, a Pork Pâté

Cretons, a potted meat similar to pork pâté, can be prepared several days ahead and kept refrigerated until the big day. It's a very traditional French Canadian appetizer and should be served with crusty French bread.

1 pound	500 g	pork fat
1 ½ pounds	750 g	ground lean pork
1 cup	250 mL	fine bread crumbs
1	1	large onion, diced
1 cup	250 mL	boiling water
1 teaspoon	5 mL	dried parsley
½ teaspoon	2 mL	cinnamon
½ teaspoon	2 mL	nutmeg
¼ teaspoon	1 mL	allspice
¼ teaspoon	1 mL	cloves
1 teaspoon	5 mL	salt
¼ teaspoon	1 mL	pepper

Dice pork fat. Place in heavy saucepan and cook slowly until browned and crispy. Remove bits.

Add ground pork, bread crumbs, onion, garlic, water, parsley, spices and seasonings to the fat remaining in saucepan. Simmer, covered, for 2 hours, stirring occasionally. Chill.

Line 2-cup (500 L) bowl or earthenware crock with plastic wrap.

Spoon mixture into bowl, packing down well. Chill for at least several more hours before serving.

To serve, invert on serving plate and remove covering.

Supply knives, crackers, French bread and good company.

Makes about 2 cups (500 mL).

Special Pastry for Tourtière

2 cups	500 mL	flour
2 teaspoons	10 mL	baking powder
1 teaspoon	5 mL	salt
⅓ cup	75 mL	butter
½ cup	125 mL	shortening
⅓-½ cup	75-125 mL	cold water
1 tablespoon	15 mL	vinegar

Combine flour, baking powder and salt. With hands, work in butter and shortening.

Combine water and vinegar and stir into the flour mixture.

Turn out onto floured board and knead for about 1 minute. Form into ball, wrap in wax paper and chill.

To use, roll out on floured board to fit pie pan.

Tourtière

Tourtiére started as a French Canadian treat but has spread to all parts of the country now – especially at Christmas time when it's served as a lunch or supper dish. Sometimes miniature Tourtières made in tart pans are served as appetizers at winter parties.

		Tourtière pastry for 2-crust pie (page 191)
1¾ pounds	875 g	ground pork
2	2	medium onions, chopped
1	1	garlic clove, minced
1 cup	250 mL	water
1 teaspoon	5 mL	salt
1 teaspoon	5 mL	dry mustard
¾ teaspoon	3 mL	sage OR savory
½ teaspoon	2 mL	thyme
¼ teaspoon	1 mL	pepper
¼ teaspoon	1 mL	nutmeg
1½ tablespoons	25 mL	flour

For Glaze:

1	1	egg white, slightly beaten
1 tablespoon	15 mL	water

Preheat oven to 400°F (200°C).

Prepare special Tourtière pastry from page 191.

Line bottom of pie plate.

Cook ground pork in frying pan until it loses pink color. Push to side (or remove temporarily) and sauté onion and garlic. Drain off excess fat.

Put meat back in pan if it was removed; add water, salt, dry mustard

(Continued on next page.)

(Continued)

and seasonings. Cover. Simmer 15 to 20 minutes. Sprinkle with flour and simmer another 2 to 3 minutes until mixture thickens slightly.

Fill pastry-lined pie plate with meat mixture. Cover top with more pastry. Seal edges and cut slits in top for steam to escape.

To make glaze, beat egg white and water slightly, brush mixture over top of pastry.

Bake for 20 minutes or until browned.

Several pies may be made at once and frozen unbaked. Allow about 40 to 50 minutes to bake a frozen meat pie.

Catsup Rouge Aux Fruits, A Fruit Chili

This is an old Canadian recipe also know as Fruit Chili. It's delicious with cold meats, meat pies, and fried chicken.

4 x 19 ounces	4 x 540 mL	tomatoes (4 cans)
6	6	onions
2 x 14 ounces	2 x 398 mL	peaches (2 cans)
2 x 14 ounces	2 x 398 mL	pears (2 cans)
3	3	large apples
3	3	red peppers
3	3	green peppers
2 cups	500 mL	white vinegar
4 cups	1 L	sugar
1 tablespoon	15 mL	salt
2 tablespoons	30 mL	pickling spice

Chop tomatoes, onions, peaches, pears, apples and peppers and place in heavy saucepan. Add vinegar, sugar and salt.

Tie spices into small cotton bag and add to mixture.

Simmer uncovered for 2 to 3 hours. Mixture should be thick.

Remove spice bag. Spoon catsup into sterilized jars. Cover and store in refrigerator.

Yields 8 to 9 pints (4 L).

Note: Instead of canned peaches and pears, you could use 6 fresh peaches, 6 fresh pears.

Creamy Coleslaw

This versatile coleslaw goes well with beef, ham or any number of cold meats. It's pretty as well as practical with bits of red apple mixed in with the green cabbage and celery.

6 cups	1.5 L	shredded cabbage
1	1	apple
1 cup	250 mL	thinly sliced celery
1 cup	250 mL	mayonnaise
2 teaspoons	10 mL	prepared mustard
3 tablespoons	45 mL	sugar
1½ tablespoons	25 mL	vinegar
1 teaspoon	5 mL	salt

Prepare cabbage. Wash but do not peel apple. Cut in small thin slices. Slice celery. Combine in large bowl.

Mix remaining ingredients. Add to vegetables and mix well.

Cover and chill until serving time.

Serves 6 to 8.

Bûche de Noël, A Cake For Christmas

The main attraction on a festive table for Christmas Eve in Québec is a Bûche de Noël, a jelly roll cake that is artfully arranged and decorated to represent a Yule log of Christmases past. It's so lovely it's a shame to eat it!

The Jelly Roll First:

1 cup	250 mL	flour
1 teaspoon	5 mL	baking powder
½ teaspoon	2 mL	salt
3	3	eggs, at room temperature
1 cup	250 mL	sugar
⅓ cup	75 mL	hot milk
3 tablespoons	45 mL	butter OR margarine
1 teaspoon	5 mL	vanilla
¼ cup	50 mL	icing (confectioner's) sugar

Preheat oven to 375°F (190°C).

Grease 12 x 18" (30 x 45 cm) jelly-roll pan. Line with wax paper cut to fit the pan. Grease the wax paper.

Combine flour, baking powder and salt in small bowl. Set aside.

In large bowl, beat eggs on high speed of electric mixer until thick and light colored, about 5 minutes. Add sugar gradually while continuing to beat. Add dry ingredients while beating on low speed.

Heat milk almost to boiling. Add butter and vanilla. Mix lightly with batter. Spread evenly in jelly-roll pan.

Bake for about 15 minutes or until cake is golden and springs back when lightly touched.

While cake is baking, sprinkle icing sugar over surface of clean tea towel.

Remove cake from oven, loosen sides from pan and turn out on tea towel. Cut off crusts.

(Continued on next page.)

Roll up loosely inside towel, rolling from the narrow end of the cake. Cool on cake rack.

This basic jelly roll could be filled with fruit and whipped cream or lemon butter or jelly… as well as serving as the base for Bûche de Noël.

Filling and Icing For Bûche de Noël:

1 cup	250 mL	apricot OR raspberry jam
⅓ cup	75 mL	butter OR margarine
1 tablespoon	15 mL	cocoa
1 tablespoon	15 mL	strong hot coffee
1 cup	250 mL	icing (confectioner's) sugar
		boiling water, as needed
3 tablespoons	45 mL	cocoa
½ cup	125 mL	icing (confectioner's) sugar
		boiling water, again,
		as needed

Unroll cooled jelly roll and spread with jam. Roll up again. Roll may now be frosted as is, or you could cut off a slanted wedge of cake from both ends, place 1 or both on the roll to simulate branches.

Cream together butter or margarine, cocoa and coffee. Add icing sugar gradually, stirring in boiling water as needed to keep mixture soft and spreadable. Beat until completely smooth.

This icing will be rather light colored. Spread as much as needed on the ends of the cake and the cut sides of the branches. The rest of the log will be darker.

To remaining icing, add the 3 tablespoons (45 mL) cocoa, the ½ cup (125 mL) icing sugar and enough boiling water to keep the icing soft and spreadable. Spread evenly over log. With a fork, make lines the length of the roll to simulate tree bark.

Yields 12 servings.

Tarte Au Sucre

This beloved traditional pie seems too good to be true. Not only is it delicious but it's about the easiest pie to make.

		pastry for bottom crust of 9" (23 cm) pie
1½ cups	375 mL	light brown sugar
½ cup	125 mL	milk
¼ cup	50 mL	diced butter

Preheat oven to 425°F (220°C).

Prepare pastry recipe, page 165, and line bottom of pie plate.

Sprinkle sugar over crust. Do not pack. Cover with milk and dot with butter.

Bake for 10 minutes. Reduce oven temperature to 3575°F (190°C) and bake for another 15 to 20 minutes or until the crust is baked.

Remove from oven and cool. Filling thickens upon cooling.

Serve with Sweetened Whipped Cream, page 35, or Homemade Ice Cream, page 15.

Ontario

Tastes of the land... and its history

Emotion built the province of Ontario – in particular, the emotion known as loyalty. If thousands of American citizens hadn't felt such a loyalty to their native England, they wouldn't have packed up kith and kin and moved to Ontario, there to be as loyal to Britain as they pleased.

It all happened during the American Revolution when the majority of American citizens decided they wanted independence rather than the continued imperial rule of England. Those who disagreed with this idea were invited to leave – and many found refuge in Britain's colonies to the north, in Canada. In 1784, as many as 10,000 Loyalists came to the area now known as Ontario, a wilderness of forests and lakes, penetrated only by Indians, missionaries and fur traders.

The new colonists were allotted farms along the St. Lawrence River, on the Bay of Quinte or near the Niagara Peninsula, and provided with an axe, a hoe and basic tools to start breaking land and building shelters. At first, the British government provided food rations of "one pound of flour and 12 ounces of pork for one pound of less-popular beef per adult, per week with half rations for the children...".[1]

However, rations were never adequate, crops often failed, the work was back breaking. It was a very difficult time for the transplanted settlers.

On top of which they found themselves living under French rule and custom. Even though the colony of Québec had been conquered by the British, there were still many remnants of the previous rule. The Loyalists complained that they hadn't left the United States to come to a French country. They were looking for a colony with British traditions, so Britain finally created Upper Canada for the loyalists and Lower Canada for the French.

By 1812, as many as 100,000 people were working together to build a nation: clearing forests, running sawmills, gristmills and blacksmith shops, baking bread in outdoor ovens and Johnny Cake in bake kettles over the fireplace, preserving wild berries and making cheese and butter.

Peace ended when the United States, angered by British policies declared war on Britain and sent troops to attack Canadian border settlements. The local militia, British troops and Loyal Indians held them off until the war ended in 1814.

Now came an even greater influx of settlers. Mennonites from Pennsylvania drove their Conestoga wagons into the interior. Thousands came from England, Ireland, Scotland and the United States. Log shanties were built with floors of split logs or hard-packed earth. Outhouses, grain barns, piggeries, outdoor bake ovens, smokehouses and icehouses were added as the settlers became established.

The preparation of food and shelter became part of the social life: logging bees, stumping bees, ploughing bees, quilting bees, corn husking bees. Anna Leveridge described her part in an 1883 bee: "We had a logging bee last week… I had plenty of cooking, about 23 folks to dinner and supper. I had to set one table out of doors. We got on well, had fresh pork fried and mashed potatoes, beans, rice pudding, rhubarb tarts, besides frying 4 dozen eggs."[2]

Naturally, as the population grew, the settlement wanted more autonomy in government. Together with three other colonies, it became one of the founding provinces of the Dominion of Canada at the time of Confederation in 1867. Upper Canada was renamed Ontario.

Life didn't get any easier. One pioneer recalled in her diary from 1895 that "Had a pretty dull day, washed all the forenoon besides chasing pigs, cows and horses. Got dinner ready and had a quarrel with both Edith and Ma about the Almighty doing all things well. 'He hasn't done anything for me', so I said and got into a devil of a row. After dinner I didn't do anything worth mentioning till night… I went into the garden and found the geese had eaten all my flowers which made me boil and I boiled over. I settled them and went to bed."[3]

Immigrants continued to come in waves, first from the British Isles and the United States, then from Europe, the West Indies and East Asia. Altogether, they made Ontario the most heavily populated province in Canada and gave her cities a lively cosmopolitan flavor.

Ontario's food traditions took root with the Loyalists but branched out very quickly with the arrival of newcomers from all over the world. Too, the proximity of the United States and its blend of peoples added to the Ontario mix. A visitor in Ontario can dine at a restaurant serving exotic international food, and then go down the road and buy apple butter, all within a few miles.

It's a marvelous mix, rich and varied.

Celebrate the foods of Ontario!

Ontario Sunday Dinner

Spring, summer and fall were filled with work for the early settlers of Ontario – planting crops, caring for them, clearing land, harvesting. It was only in the fall that a little leisure crept into the scheme of things – time to visit and enjoy the fruits of the summer-long labour.

When the trees turned yellow and crimson, when the corn was picked and processed, when the gallons of apple butter were put down, when the first hog was slaughtered and safely in the smokehouse... then could folks think about visiting. When the frost came on the pumpkin and when it was time to change the muslin for flannel, thoughts turned to gentler things. Then was the time to hitch up the horses to the sleigh and take off on snow-covered tracks to... SUNDAY DINNER.

This special Sunday dinner is a celebration of days gone by. It features Crown Roast of Pork, and updated version of the old favorite roast pork accompanied by apple butter, an extra spicy version of apple sauce. Suggested vegetables include Corn Pudding, Glazed Carrots and Onions, and Green Beans with Lemon Butter.

Finally, a choice of desserts: a Layer Cake with a wonderful difference, and Baked Apples with Mincemeat. Both delicious, both worthy of their position as the finale of an elegant Sunday dinner!

MENU
● ● ● ●

Crown Roast of Pork with Sausage Stuffing
Apple Butter
Corn Pudding
Glazed Carrots and Onions
Green Beans with Lemon Butter
Waldorf Salad
Blitz Torte Cake
Baked Apples with Mincemeat
Lost Lemon Cake

Crown Roast of Pork

This elegant roast reflects the way we were – in early Ontario, and the way we are – in modern Ontario!

6 pounds	3 kg	crown roast of pork
1 pound	500 g	sausage meat
½ cup	125 mL	chopped onion
4 cups	1 L	bread crumbs
1 teaspoon	5 mL	salt
¼ teaspoon	1 mL	pepper
1 teaspoon	5 mL	sage OR savory
½ teaspoon	2 mL	thyme

Preheat oven to 325°F (160°C).

Order crown roast of pork from your butcher, allows 1-1½ ribs per person. Trim off any excess fat.

To make the stuffing, sauté sausage meat until the pinkness disappears, breaking meat up with a fork. Remove sausage meat to a bowl. Sauté onion in the remaining fat.

Toss bread crumbs with salt, pepper and other seasonings. Add sausage meat and onion. Mix lightly.

Stand roast, ribs up, on a rack in a shallow roasting pan. Place 2 layers of foil under roast, to make sure stuffing doesn't fall out.

Fill center of roast with stuffing. Place small pieces of foil over rib ends to prevent burning.

Roast for 3 hours or until meat thermometer inserted in the meaty portion reaches 170°F (80°C).

Lift roast to a platter and garnish with sprigs of parsley. Carve from the top down between ribs, serving 1 rib per person along with a spoonful of stuffing.

Serves 8 to 10.

Apple Butter

*Apple butter or apple sauce is traditionally served with roast pork,
pork chops and sausages -- also with muffins, biscuits, apples and
gingerbread. Canadian housewives in apple-growing regions used to
put up gallons of apple butter for winter use.*

2 cups	500 mL	apple cider
8 cups	2 L	sliced apples
½ cup	125 mL	sugar
1 teaspoon	5 mL	cinnamon

Simmer apple cider 5 to 10 minutes to reduce it. Peel, cone and slide
the apples. Simmer in the cider, uncovered, until mixture is thick and
mushy. Stir frequently.

Add sugar and cinnamon. Cool.

Store in refrigerator until used.

*Note: Sour apples are best for this recipe. If you find really sour ones,
you may have to adjust the sugar.*

Corn Pudding

This is not a dessert, despite the name. This is a vegetable dish to be served with beef, pork or fowl.

3	3	eggs
4½ tablespoons	70 mL	flour
2 x 14 ounces	2 x 398 mL	creamed corn (2 cans)
14 ounces	398 mL	niblet corn (1 can)
1½ cups	375 mL	milk
¾ cup	175 mL	grated Cheddar cheese
2 teaspoons	10 mL	salt
¼ teaspoon	1 mL	pepper

Preheat oven to 325°F (160°C).

Beat eggs slightly. Whisk in flour. Add corns, milk, cheese, salt and pepper.

Pour into greased casserole dish and bake for 1-1½ hours or until set – it depends on depth of baking dish.

Serves 8.

Glazed Onions and Carrots

An easy delicious vegetable dish can be tucked into the oven to slow cook along with the rest of the meal.

6 cups	1.5 L	onions, cut in wedges
6 cups	1.5 L	carrots, cut in rounds
2 tablespoons	30 mL	butter OR margarine
2 tablespoons	30 mL	honey
½ teaspoon	2 mL	salt

Preheat oven to 325°F (160°C).

Place vegetables in greased baking dish, onions on one side, carrots on the other.

Heat butter or margarine with honey and salt. Drizzle over the vegetables.

Cover tightly and bake for 1½ to 2 hours, or until tender.

Serves 8.

Green Beans with Lemon

Sometimes the simplest things taste the best. This is certainly simple and it certainly tastes good!

1½ pounds	750 g	green beans
2 tablespoons	30 mL	butter
1 tablespoon	15 mL	lemon juice
		salt and pepper to taste

Cook beans in salted boiling water until just tender, about 5 minutes. Drain.

Melt butter, mix with lemon juice. Drizzle over the beans and toss lightly. Season to taste.

Serves 8.

Waldorf Salad

Apples are a perfect complement for pork – in more ways than one. You could serve the Apple butter or the Waldorf Salad, one of the prettiest salads going!

3	3	medium red apples
½ cup	125 mL	dates OR walnuts
1 cup	250 mL	sliced celery
1 cup	250 mL	whipping cream
½ cup	125 mL	mayonnaise
		chopped walnuts for garnish (optional)

Baked Apples with Mincemeat

Since the first Acadians planted apple trees in Maritimes, apples have been an integral part of Canada's cuisine. The following recipe is a delicious variation on baked apples, this one with mincemeat in the core.

4	4	large cooking apples
½ cup	125 mL	mincemeat
½ cup	125 mL	brown sugar
1 teaspoon	5 mL	cinnamon
1 cup	250 mL	water

Preheat oven to 350°F (180°C).

Wash apples and core. Remove 1 row of peel around middle of outside to allow for expansion. Place apples in baking dish big enough so apples don't touch. Fill centers with mincemeat.

Combine sugar, cinnamon and water. Pour over apples. Cover with lid or foil.

Bake for 30 minutes, or until just tender. Baking time varies with variety of apple.

Serve warm with pouring cream, whipped cream or ice cream.

Blitz Torte Cake

In earlier times when men and women didn't watch their waistlines with such intensity, a good housewife felt she had to produce at least 2, preferably 3, desserts for a dinner party. This was a favorite.

½ cup	125 mL	butter
½ cup	125 mL	sugar
4	4	eggs, separated
1 teaspoon	5 mL	vanilla
½ cup	125 mL	milk
1 cup	250 mL	flour
1 teaspoon	5 mL	baking powder
¼ teaspoon	1 mL	salt
1 cup	250 mL	sugar

Preheat oven to 350°F (180°C).

Grease two, 9" (23 cm) round cake pans. Sprinkle lightly with flour. Cream butter and ½ cup (125 mL) sugar until fluffy.

Separate eggs and set whites aside. Add yolks to the creamed mixture and beat until light and creamy. Add vanilla.

Mix flour, baking powder and salt. Fold dry ingredients alternately with milk into the creamed mixture.   Divide evenly into the 2 pans.

To make the meringue, beat reserved egg whites until stiff. Gradually add 1 cup (250 mL) sugar and beat continuously until sugar is dissolved and meringue will stand in peaks. Spread on top of batter in pans.

Bake for 25 to 30 minutes or until toothpick inserted into cake comes out clean. Remove from oven and cool in pans.

To finish, place 1 cake layer, meringue side down on a cake plate. Spread with half of Whipped Cream Filling or Lemon Filling, recipes below. Place second layer with meringue on top. Spread with remaining filling.

(Continued on next page.)

(Continued)

Whipped Cream Filling:

1 cup	250 mL	whipping cream
2 tablespoons	30 mL	sugar
1 teaspoon	5 mL	vanilla

Whip cream until stiff. Fold in sugar and vanilla.

Lemon Satin Filling:

1 cup	250 mL	whipping cream
⅓ cup	75 mL	icing (confectioner's) sugar
2 tablespoons	30 mL	lemon juice
1 teaspoon	5 mL	grated lemon rind

Place all ingredients in a mixing bowl and beat until thick.

The Lost Lemon Cake

Make the Yellow Layer cake in 2 layers. When cake has cooled, cut each later in half with a bread knife so that you have 4 layers. Place first layer on a cake plate, spread with ⅓ Lemon Satin Filling, page 209. Cover with second cake layer and over it spread another ⅓ of Lemon Filling. Cover with fourth layer. Frost top and sides with Lemon Butter Icing.

Yellow Layer Cake

2 ¼ cups	550 mL	cake flour
1 ¼ cups	300 mL	berry sugar
2 teaspoons	10 mL	baking powder
½ teaspoon	2 mL	salt
2	2	egg yolks
½ cup	125 mL	soft butter
⅔ cup	150 mL	milk
2	2	egg whites, unbeaten
⅓ cup	75 mL	milk
1 teaspoon	5 mL	vanilla

Preheat oven to 375°F (190°C).

Sift cake flour before measuring. Stir with sugar, baking powder and salt. Add egg yolks, soft butter or margarine and ⅔ cup (150 mL) milk. Beat until smooth, about 1½ minutes on medium. Add egg whites, remaining milk and vanilla. Beat another minute until smooth.

Spread into two 8" (20 cm) greased and floured round layer-cake pans and bake for about 25 to 35 minutes or until a toothpick inserted into center comes out clean.

Cool on racks for 10 minutes. Turn out and cool to room temperature before filling and frosting.

(Continued on next page.)

(Continued)

Lemon Butter Icing

There are three secrets to achieving a light fluffy icing: beat, beat, beat.

½ cup	125 mL	butter OR margarine
1	1	grated lemon rind
2 cups	500 mL	icing (confectioner's) sugar
2 tablespoons	30 mL	lemon juice
4-5 tablespoons	60-75 mL	boiling water

Cream butter or margarine. Add lemon rind. Add half of sugar and beat until smooth. Add remaining sugar and continue beating. Add lemon juice and enough boiling water to make soft icing. Beat well.

This makes enough icing for 2-layer cake or 9 x 13" (22 x 33 cm) pan cake. Cut recipe in half for smaller cake.

Notes

Manitoba
Tastes of the land... and its history

A fortune could be made from beaver pelts, and with that objective in mind, Europeans began venturing into the great North West of North America.

The Hudson's Bay Company from England obtained trading rights to all lands draining into the Hudson Bay and operated trading posts on its rim. Supplies were brought once a year by ship from England and augmented by locally caught fish and game.

Montreal was headquarters for the rival company, the Northwest Company. From there, voyageurs navigated canoes loaded with trading goods over a tortuous inland water route. As they moved west, they lived on dried peas and corn and salt pork, adding wild rice, dried buffalo meat and pemmican.

Eventually, the two companies had a string of posts across the country from which they traded cloth, shirts, beads, blankets, guns and ammunition for prime furs. Competiton between them was ruthless until they merged in 1821 as the Hudson's Bay Company. Fort Garry, located at the forks of the Red and Assiniboine Rivers, became the major administration and provisioning post.

Living conditions at outlying forts were spartan but at Fort Garry the traders lived comfortably. Charles Mair wrote of his visit: "We had a pleasant stay at Fort Garry and received all sorts of entertainment. They live like princes here. Just fancy what we had at a dinner party. Oyster Soup, White Fish, Roast Beef, Roast Prairie chicken, green peas, tomatoes stewed and stewed gooseberries, Plum Pudding, Blanc Mange, raisins, nuts of all kinds, coffee, port and sherry, Brandy Punch and cigars, concluding with whist until 4 o'clock a.m. There is a dinner for you, in the heart of a continent, with Indian skin lodges within a stone's throw."[1]

The first farming settlement in the area was established by Lord Selkirk in 1812 when he led a group of Scots to the Red River area. They became known as the Selkirk settlers or the Red River settlers.

Not far away was a settlement of Metis (children of European fathers and Indian mothers) who lived by hunting and performing various tasks for the fur traders. Twice a year, they traveled to the prairies on organized buffalo hunts – men, women, children, horses, oxen and Red River carts. The men did the hunting and the women and children dressed the carcasses. Weeks later when they had sufficient supplies of meat, dried meat, pemmican, pickled buffalo tongues, hides and buffalo bladders filled with melted fat, the carts returned home.

After beaver hats went out of fashion in Europe, the fur trade declined. Canada purchased Rupert's Land from the Hudson's Bay Company and the Red River settlement became the province of Manitoba in 1870. Within a few years, Fort Garry became the city of Winnipeg.

The Metis were not so thrilled with all this political activity – the influx of settlers, the land surveys that were being done, the new political system. Many felt cheated of their rights and packed up to move further west. Eventually, this discontent was to erupt into the Riel Rebellion of 1885.

Meanwhile, the province of Manitoba was filling up with settlers from all over the world. Mennonites moved onto the open prairies. Icelandic settlers chose the area around Gimli on Lake Winnipeg, because if afforded them many of the advantages of their original home. Jewish immigrants escaped the pogroms of Europe and gratefully settled in Winnipeg. Ukrainians, Poles, Germans and more Scots moved onto the open prairie lands, grateful for the fact that the land was easy to clear but a little frightened, sometimes by its vastness. Other settlers came from eastern Canada and the United States.

Winnipeg experienced a railroad building and real estate boom. Fortunes were made, and a certain level of "society" was established with its attendant balls and theatricals, concerts, whist parties, skating parties, garden parties... all of which meant dainty sandwiches and tea and lemonade and cakes and all the finer things of life.

Meanwhile, out on the prairies and parklands, farmers struggled to get crops planted, crops which included cabbage, corn, peas, beans, turnips, potatoes and grains. Their wives sought out berries of the land – Saskatoons, raspberries, strawberries, chokecherries, gooseberries, currants and cranberries. Eventually, they too secured a food supply in this new land.

Celebrate the foods of Manitoba!

Manitoba Dinner at the Fort

Manitoba's history is filled with the romance of the fur trade, the time when voyageurs paddled down the St. Lawrence River and across the lake country. As they moved by water and by land, they looked forward to reaching what is now Manitoba for here they could purchase wild rice, buffalo meat and pemmican from the Indians. Here for the hunting were ducks, geese, pigeons and prairie chickens.

Fur traders built the first Fort Garry (now Winnipeg) at the forks of the Red and Assinboine Rivers, and York Factory on the rim of Hudson Bay. Another fort, which became known as Lower Fort Garry, was built down river from the first Fort Garry and today is an important history site.

The menu for our dinner at the fort is an elegant meal, reminiscent of some of the special meals served at the fort. It starts with a simple tasty salad, followed by the main course, glazed Duck with Currant Sauce.

Wild rice grows particularly well in Manitoba which is why it's included in the Fort Dinner. With it, we suggest you serve Sweet and Sour Red Cabbage, a great taste and color choice!

Pie was always a favorite of Canada's pioneers and two of the best are included here – Mock-Cherry Pie and Mince Apple Pie.

As well, we've included a recipe for Winnipeg Gold Eye, the most famous and delicious accident to ever come out of Winnipeg!

MENU
● ● ● ●

Romaine and Orange Salad... page 56
Glazed Duck with Currant Sauce
Wild Rice
Sweet and Sour Cabbage
Buttered Green Peas
Mock-Cherry Pie OR
Hot Mince Apple Pie with Ice Cream
(And just for good measure... Winnipeg Goldeye)

Glazed Duck with Currant Sauce

*Fur traders looked forward to the coming of spring when wild fowl
provided a change from fish and buffalo. Geese and ducks of Canada's
north still provide a change – and a feast – for Canadian diners!*

4	4	wild ducks OR
2	2	domestic ducks
		salt and pepper
½ teaspoon	2 mL	sage
1 cup	250 mL	red currant jelly
1 cup	250 mL	beef broth
½ cup	125 mL	Madeira wine
		OR orange juice
½ teaspoon	2 mL	ginger

Preheat oven to 350°F (180°C).

Rinse and dry ducks inside and out. Sprinkle with salt and pepper.
Rub sage inside cavities. Roast on a rack in a shallow roasting pan for
2-2½ hours or until the drumstick wriggles easily when moved.

Prick surface to rid duck of excess fat. Drain fat from roasting pan.

Melt red or black currant jelly, brush on ducks and continue roasting
for ½ hour. Brush surface with jelly several times. Remove ducks to a
platter. Drain fat from roasting pan again.

Add broth, wine or orange juice and ginger to residue in the pan.
Simmer and stir.

Carve ducks. If ducks are wild, it might be easier to cut into serving
portions in the kitchen, as the wild ducks are sometimes small and
hard to handle. Spoon sauce over portions.

Serves 4.

Sweet and Sour Red Cabbage

This vegetable dish is excellent with wild game, poultry and ham.
Allow at least 1 cup (250 mL) per person. Cabbage can be prepared
ahead and reheated.

6 cups	1.5 L	chopped red cabbage
		water
6 tablespoons	90 mL	brown sugar
6 tablespoons	90 mL	vinegar
		salt and freshly
		ground black pepper

Place chopped cabbage in frying pan. Add just enough water to cover bottom. Mix sugar and vinegar and stir in.

Cover and cook over medium heat, stirring frequently. Cabbage should be slightly crisp when done.

Serves 4.

Wild Rice

This distinctive flavor of wild rice combines particularly well with game and fowl. It's actually a cereal grain like oats and wheat but it is called rice because it puffs up like rice when it cooks and it grows in rice-like settings.

1 cup	250 mL	wild rice
		boiling water to cover
3 tablespoons	45 mL	butter
⅓ cup	75 mL	chopped onion
½ teaspoon	2 mL	sage, thyme, salt EACH
		dash freshly ground pepper
10 ounces	284 mL	beef broth (1 can)
1 cup	250 mL	water

Preheat oven to 350°F (180°C).

In colander or steamer, wash rice under running water. Place in saucepan, cover with boiling water and let stand 5 minutes. Drain and cover with boiling water again, and let stand another 5 minutes. (This soaking removes all weedy flavors.) Drain again.

In small frying pan, melt butter and sauté onions. Place rice, onions, seasonings, broth and water in greased casserole dish.

Bake for 60 minutes or until rice is tender but not mushy.

Mock-Cherry Pie

Because cranberries were so plentiful in the early days, housewives learned to use them in all sorts of ways – including ways that hid their true identity. Thus did they develop one of the most delicious and best loved pies ever... the Mock Cherry!

		pastry for a 2-crust 9" (23 cm) pie
2 cups	500 mL	cranberries
1 cup	250 mL	raisins
¾ cup	175 mL	sugar
2 tablespoons	30 mL	flour
1 cup	250 mL	water
½ teaspoon	2 mL	vanilla
1 tablespoon	15 mL	butter
		milk and sugar for glaze

Preheat oven to 400°F (200°C).

Prepare pastry recipe, page 165, and line pie plate.

In saucepan, combine cranberries, raisins, sugar and flour. Add water. Bring to a boil and simmer until thickened, about 5 minutes. Add vanilla and butter. Pour into pastry shell.

Cut ½" (1.5 cm) pastry strips and arrange over top to from a lattice crust. Brush pastry strips lightly with milk and sprinkle with sugar.

Bake for 35 to 45 minutes or until browned. Serve warm or cold with whipped cream or ice cream.

Mince Apple Pie

There was a time when mincemeat actually included meat, and when every homemaker made her own mixture. However, mincemeat doesn't actually have meat in it any more and very few of us make our own. Still, the fruit and spice mixture makes a wonderful pie and is a traditional Canadian treat!

		pastry for a 2-crust 9" (23 cm) pie
3	3	apples
3-4 cups	750 mL-1 L	mincemeat
2 tablespoons	30 mL	brandy

Preheat oven to 400°F (200°C).

Prepare pastry recipe, page 165, and line bottom of pie plate.

Peel, core and chop apples. Spread on bottom of crust. Mix mincemeat and brandy and spread over apples. Cover with top crust. Be sure to make 2 or 3 slits for steam to escape.

Bake for 35 to 40 minutes or until nicely browned.

Serve in small wedges with Sweetened Whipped Cream, page 35, or Homemade Ice Cream, page 15.

Serves 8 to 10.

Winnipeg Goldeye

One story about the origin of the famous Winnipeg Goldeye dates back to 1886 when an early settler is said to have purchased smoked goldeye from local Indians. His family liked them so much that he began to catch and smoke his own, giving them a light smoke over reddish yellow twigs, as was the Indian custom. Alas, one day he forgot his fish over the burning twigs and they cooked more than he had intended. Imagine his surprise when he tasted them and discovered that they were better than ever.

His mistake became the most famous specialty food from Manitoba, featured, for years, in the spiffy dining cars of the Canadian Pacific Railway.

To enjoy and serve your own Goldeye… you'll have to buy some unless you have a smokehouse in the backyard. Since it is already cooked, you need only heat it. This can be done a couple of ways:

By frying: Pour small amount of water into frying pan and bring to boil. Place Goldeye in water and heat through, approximately 4 minutes per side. Peel skin off as they heat. Serve with butter and lemon.

By steaming in the oven: Preheat oven to 350°F (180°C). Place fish in baking dish. Add small amount of water. Cover with foil and allow to steam in oven for approximately 30 minutes. Remove skin and serve with butter and lemon.

Notes

Saskatchewan
Tastes of the land... and its history

The Canadian prairies are great providers of food and have been throughout man's history. Today, it is fields and fields of grain. At one time, herds of buffalo stretched as far as the eye could see, making easy dining for the Prairie Indians. Dried buffalo meat and concentrated pemmican made it possible for European fur traders to travel immense distances quickly with little chance of starvation. Buffalo were so plentiful that fur trading posts were set up to process buffalo meat and fat, and ship it by canoe elsewhere.

Alas, the herds of buffalo were overhunted and the trade in furs declined. When the Canadian Government purchased the territory in 1969 the prairies were open for new business and new people.

So, the government passed the Dominion Land Act which allowed settlers to obtain a quarter of a section of land, a homestead, for $10.00, provided that the settler in question lived on the land for a specified time and improved upon it. Advertisements were distributed throughout Europe to find willing takers, and railway building was accelerated in order to be able to bring the new settlers to the new settlements.

It worked – settlers flocked to Canada's Midwest with $10.00 and a dream – the dream of their own land and independence.

Life was hard and work backbreaking. Some homes were built of chunks of prairie sod cut from slough bottoms. Some were logs. A few were lumber but you had to have money for that! The grind of work was occasionally broken by church suppers, picnics, card parties, and sports days.

The first settlers ate salt pork, beans and potatoes until the wheat fields, vegetable gardens, cattle herds and chicken flocks became established.

The year revolved around seeding and harvesting. When crops were ripe, threshing outfits moved from farm to farm with a crew of up to 20 men who hauled the bundles of grain and pitched them into the giant threshing machines where the kernels of grain were separated from the straw. The housewife fed the hungry men three meals a day along with an afternoon lunch. Food had to be the best she could offer – big roasts of ham, beef or pork, fried chicken, fresh garden vegetables, bread and buns, pickles and preserves, pies, cakes, cookies and doughnuts.

One young housewife wanted to impress the threshers with her cooking. She made six raisin pies (they were most common as fresh fruit soon spoilt without refrigeration). The noon whistle sounded before the potatoes were drained and hurriedly she placed her half dozen pies on the table along with plates of bread, butter and beet pickles. When she came from the kitchen with a platter of meat and a bowl of potatoes, there were neither pies nor pickles left. The hungry threshers had 'fallen to' what was set before them.

When Saskatchewan was made a province in 1905, Regina became the capital city. In contrast to life on the farm, Regina was a social metropolis with receptions and state balls at Government House, dances at the Mounted Police barracks, and ladies who left visiting cards on silver trays announcing "At Homes".

A strong sense of mutual support and cooperation developed among the people. Prairie farms grew rich fields of wheat which stretched as far as the eye could see. It seemed as if nothing could go wrong.

But, of course, something could, and did. Drought and depression delivered a double whammy in the 1920's and 1930's. The pioneers were devastated. One prairie wife recalled, "There was no water, no toilet, no bath, no washing machine, no sink, no vacation, no spending money, no jobs for the young, and the nearest doctor was seven miles away by horse."

In many homes, food was limited to what the farmer could produce – home-ground flour, boiled-wheat porridge, garden vegetables that survived the drought, eggs, home-cured meat, coffee made from roasted barley, dandelion roots or dried bread crusts. Many town people and farm folk depended on relief and shipments of food from other provinces.

There was so little currency that doctors and ministers of the church were often paid with produce. One year almost every parishioner at a certain church left turnips at the parsonage – in lieu of money. The minister said nothing but invited the church officials to his home for a meal. His wife served: Turnip Soup, Turnip Loaf, Mashed Turnips, Turnip Salad and Turnip Pie. History does not record whether the church officials found some money after all.

The Great Depression lasted until 1939; then the farms began to flourish again. Later, the discovery of oil and gas, potash and uranium strengthened the economic base and helped make Saskatchewan a well-to-do province. Its fields of ripening wheat have earned it the name, "The Great Bread Basket of the World".

Celebrate the foods of Saskatchewan!

Saskatchewan Harvest Dinner

Even if you're not a farmer in Saskatchewan at harvest time, you feel as if you should be. Those wide-open skies, the sunshine filtering through the dust of harvesting operations, the feeling of accomplishment that another harvest is finished... everyone is affected by it. And homemakers, as if by some genetic urging, make larger meals than usual, as if they were out there cooking for the threshers just like mother and grandmother did.

The menu for the Harvest Supper is similar to what might have been served to the threshers or to people who came to other community celebrations such as the Ladies-Aid Suppers, Chicken Suppers, and the annual Bazaar. The food was always basic, abundant, and very tasty. The best of what the prairie kitchens had to offer.

Start with ham glazed with a tart Mustard Sauce that lifts the ham way above the ordinary. Serve with Scalloped Potatoes – where would community meals be without this old and delicious standby? And, speaking of standbys, we've included a wonderful recipe for that old favorite – Coleslaw. Top off the first course with Buttermilk Biscuits – a handy recipe for all kinds of reasons and seasons!

For dessert, we've selected Sour Cream Raisin Pie and Spice Cake with Raisin Icing – both full of that down-home goodness that's hard to beat!

MENU
● ● ● ●
Mustard-Glazed Ham
Scalloped Potatoes
Green Beans with Lemon Butter... page 206
Old-Fashioned Coleslaw
Buttermilk Biscuits
Sour Cream Raisin Pie
Spice Cake with Raisin Icing... page 144
Date Squares

Mustard-Glazed Ham

Baked ham is a party food in most parts of Canada but particularly popular on the prairies. This recipe includes a delicious mustard glaze and sauce, a nice way to serve this old favorite. By the way, if you find ham too salty for your liking, pour 7-Up over the ham before baking and leave to soak for about 4 hours. The ham will be delicious.

6-8 pounds	3-4 kg	ham, bone-in
2 cups	500 mL	brown sugar
2 tablespoons	30 mL	flour
½ teaspoon	2 mL	salt
½ cup	125 mL	dry mustard
1 cup	250 mL	vinegar
1 cup	250 mL	water
2	2	beef bouillon cubes
4	4	egg yolks, beaten

Preheat oven to 400°F (200°C).

In small saucepan, mix sugar, flour, salt and mustard. Stir in vinegar, water and crushed beef bouillon cubes. Simmer for few minutes, then stir a little of the hot mixture into beaten egg yolks.

Add egg mixture back to mustard mixture and cook while stirring for 1 to 2 minutes. Remove from heat and cool slightly.

Trim excess fat from ham. Score remaining fat, making a diamond pattern over all. Spoon glaze over surface. Bake for 45 minutes to set glaze.

Turn oven down to 325°F (160°C) and continue baking for about 2½ hours or until ham registers 160°F (75°C) on meat thermometer. Spoon more glaze over ham several times during baking period. Serve extra glaze as Mustard Sauce.

Serves 12 to 14.

Scalloped Potatoes

On the prairies, scalloped potatoes are the favorite casserole to serve at community or church suppers. They're good with cold meat, ham, and beef.

8 cups	2 L	thinly sliced potatoes
1	1	large onion, chopped
4 tablespoons	60 mL	flour
4 cups	1 L	milk
2½ teaspoons	12 mL	salt
		dash freshly ground pepper
3 tablespoons	45 mL	butter

Preheat oven to 325°F (160°C).

In shallow baking dish, combine sliced raw potatoes, onions and flour, mixing carefully until potatoes are all evenly coated with flour.

Combine milk, salt and pepper. Pour over potatoes. Dot with butter.

Bake for 1½ to 2 hours or until tender.

Serves 12 to 14.

Buttermilk Biscuits

These light tender tasty biscuits, a variation of tea biscuits or baking powder biscuits, are one of Canada's favorite quick breads. They are very obliging – work very well for breakfast, brunch, lunch, dinner or snacks – and they will keep fresh and delicious for several days.

2 cups	500 mL	flour
1½ tablespoons	25 mL	sugar
4 teaspoons	20 mL	baking powder
½ teaspoon	2 mL	salt
½ cup	125 mL	melted butter
1	1	egg, beaten
1 cup	250 mL	buttermilk

Preheat oven to 425°F (210°C).

Place dry ingredients in bowl.

Combine melted butter, egg and buttermilk. Add to dry ingredients and beat with electric mixer for about 2 minutes.

Turn mixture out onto well-floured board and pat or roll out about ½" (1.5 cm) thick. Cut with biscuit cutter.

Bake for 10 to 15 minutes or until lightly browned.

Yields about 24.

Old-Fashioned Coleslaw

German settlers to Canada made "Kohlslaw" by mixing shredded cabbage with a hot dressing. Cabbage was plentiful and pioneers knew that it kept the dreaded "scurvie" away. Soon, everyone was making it, using a sweet dressing when serving with turkey and ham, and a sour dressing if serving with beef. This version uses the sweet dressing.

5 cups	1.25 L	shredded cabbage
1	1	onion, finely chopped
½ cup	125 mL	vinegar
½ cup	125 mL	salad oil
¾ cup	175 mL	sugar
1 teaspoon	5 mL	salt
1 teaspoon	5 mL	dry mustard
2 teaspoons	10 mL	sesame seeds
¼ cup	50 mL	slivered almonds

Prepare cabbage and onion. Set aside.

In jar with lid, combine vinegar, oil, sugar, salt and dry mustard. Shake well.

Mix with the cabbage and onion. Marinate for several hours, stirring occasionally.

Refrigerate, covered, until time to serve. Just before serving, stir in sesame seeds and almonds.

Serves 12.

Date Squares

This cake has a moist date filling lying between crunchy oatmeal layers. It's delicious served cold for a snack or picnic food and equally delicious served warm with ice cream for a more formal dessert.

3 cups	750 mL	chopped dates
3 cups	750 mL	water
2 teaspoons	10 mL	vanilla
2 cups	500 mL	flour
2 teaspoons	10 mL	baking powder
¾ teaspoon	3 mL	salt
1¼ cups	300 mL	brown sugar
4 cups	1 L	rolled oats
1½ cups	375 mL	butter OR margarine

Preheat oven to 350°F (180°C).

To make filling, cover dates with water and cook until thick and mushy. If dates are dry, add more water. Remove from heat and add vanilla.

To make crumbs, mix flour, baking powder, salt, sugar and oats. With hands, rub in butter or margarine until mixture resembles coarse crumbs.

Pat ½ of crumb mixture into 9 x 13" (22 x 33 cm) pan.

Spread date filling over top. Spread remaining crumb mixture over dates.

Bake for 40 minutes or until lightly browned.

Sour Cream Raisin Pie

This cinnamon-spiced creamy raisin pie was a favorite in Canadian homes in years gone by when thick cream was plentiful and pie making was serious business and, happily for all of us, it has stood the test of time.

		pastry for single-crust 9" (23 cm) pie
3	3	eggs
1½ cups	375 mL	sugar
2 tablespoons	30 mL	flour
1 teaspoon	5 mL	cinnamon
½ teaspoon	2 mL	nutmeg
1 teaspoon	5 mL	salt
2 tablespoons	30 mL	whiskey OR rum
2 cups	500 mL	sour cream
1½ cups	375 mL	raisins, washed

Preheat oven to 400°F (230°C).

Prepare pastry recipe, page 165. Line bottom of pie plate.

Beat eggs, add remaining ingredients. Pour into shell.

Bake for 10 minutes, then turn oven down to 350°F (180°C) and bake for 40 minutes longer, or until pie is browned and knife blade, when inserted, comes out clean.

Serves 8

Notes

Alberta

Tastes of the land... and its history

Fur traders built Fort Edmonton on the banks of the North Saskatchewan River in the early 1800's, and from there voyageurs and fur traders traveled to the rich fur country of the Peace and Athabasca areas further north. Sometimes, the canoes and York boats loaded with supplies from the Hudson's Bay met the boats returning with full loads of pressed furs.

Hunters were engaged to keep the fort's ice house filled with buffalo meat. Indians brought fish from Lac St. Anne. Barley was grown nearby and milled into flour to make barley cakes. Bone marrow was rendered from buffalo bones for "prairie butter".

Paul Kane, the early western artist, described Christmas dinner at Fort Edmonton thus: "At the head, before Mr. Harriet, was a large dish of boiled buffalo hump; at the foot smoked a boiled buffalo calf. Start not, gentle reader, the calf is very small, and is taken from the cow by the Caesarean operation, long before it attains its full growth. This, boiled whole, is one of the most esteemed dishes amongst the epicures of the interior. My pleasing duty was to help a dish of mouffle, or dried moose nose; the gentlemen on my left distributed, with graceful impartiality, the white fish, delicately browned in buffalo marrow. The worthy priest helped the buffalo tongue, whilst Mr. Rundle cut up the beavers' tails. Nor was the other gentlemen left unemployed, as all his spare time was occupied in dissecting a roast wild goose. The center of the table was graced with piles of potatoes, turnips and bread conveniently placed, so that each would help himself without interrupting the labours of his companions. Such was our jolly Christmas dinner at Edmonton and long will it remain in our memories, although no pies or puddings, or Blanc Manges, shed their fragrance over the scene."[1]

Gradually, the village of Edmonton grew up around the fort. Well-worn trails connected with Fort Garry, now Winnipeg, some 850 miles away by Red River cart. Annie Newby Walters recalled such a trip taken in the 1880's. "The prairies were beautifully green; game was plentiful; prairie chickens and ducks shot on the way were plucked by the women as they rode along in the ox-carts, so as to be ready when camp was made."

Meanwhile, in southern Alberta, American whiskey traders began selling "rot gut" whiskey to the Blackfoot Indians so the Canadian government organized the North West Mounted police to keep law and order. They rode west and established a string of posts across the prairies and foothills. Their

first Christmas at Fort Calgary in 1875 was celebrated with a formal dinner consisting of canned oyster soup, buffalo, venison, antelope, prairie chicken, Plum Pudding, Mince Pie, nuts, candies and coffee. They lacked for nothing except vegetables, perhaps!

By this time, the buffalo were almost gone, leaving the Indians destitute and the settlers and mounties without meat. Ranchers and cowboys, hearing of the luxuriant grass lands now vacant, began trailing in cattle herds from as far away as Mexico.

At first, the countryside was one big open cattle range. Roundups were held twice a year to separate the herds in order to brand the new calves with the correct ranch brand. Chuckwagons went along to serve as kitchen, dining room and social center. From the back of the wagon, the cook turned out ranch steak, fried salt pork, beans, sourdough bread, raisin pie and black, black coffee.

In 1883, the railroad was laid through Alberta and life began to change for the big ranchers. For one thing, settlers came in wanting land for farming... and that meant fences and the end to unlimited space for ranching. Immigrants from Britain, Germany, the Ukraine, Norway, Denmark, France, Holland, Poland and the United States paid the $10.00 filing fee to take out homestead rights on a precious 160 acres of land. Towns sprang up along the railroad lines complete with hotels, blacksmith shops, lumber yards and grain elevators to service the farms.

Alberta was given provincial status in 1905 with Edmonton named the capital city.

The establishment of an oil, gas and petrochemical industry broadened the farm and ranch-based economy and brought new residents to the province, also broadening the variety of foods sold and enjoyed.

However, Albertans are above all proud of their ranch and farm-food legacy. Beef is king, as it should be in a province where cattle graze along the foothills and where June means branding. Even city cowboys know that and eat and dress accordingly!

Celebrate the foods of Alberta!

Alberta Ranchland Dinner

Albertans enjoy more "beef attacks" than residents of other provinces – partly because their province produces such excellent beef but also because many Albertans are only one generation away from the farm or ranch. They grew up with beef, they like it, that's all there is to it.

So when a big meal is planned – particularly a summer gathering – it's usually beef that is featured. When tourists come to the province, they are generally given at least one "beef and bean" feast in the great outdoors – with any luck!

A proper western outfit is not absolutely necessary, but it helps -- a plaid shirt, jeans or a fringed skirt, a Stetson, cowboy boots. Many an urban cowboy can barely move in all his or her western finery, but it's all part of the fun. Part of remembering where we came from, and what we're about to have… beef!

Start with a Baron of Beef, crusty brown on the outside, juicy pink on the inside. Serve with traditional Western Baked Beans, Creamy Coleslaw or Marinated Vegetables. Finish up with a selection of pies… just like mother's, or just like that old chuckwagon cook's, so many years ago! And for good measure, we've included a recipe for Rhubarb Crisp, another taste that's remembered fondly by many Canadians.

MENU
● ● ● ●

Baron of Beef
Western Baked Beans
Creamy Coleslaw… page 195
Marinated Onions in Sour Cream
Marinated Tomato and Onion Salad
Air Buns
Deep Apple Pie with Rum Sauce
Saskatoon Pie
Rhubarb Crisp

Baron of Beef

If you're planning a party for 40 or more, you can order yourself a whole hip of beef. Sear it on the outside and then barbecue or roast slowly for approximately 20 minutes per pound, (50 minutes per kilogram).

However, if you're not having the whole neighborhood over, you may want to use just the top part of the hip roast, otherwise known as the baron. Ask your butcher to make it into a long boneless easy-to-carve roast, resembling a rolled prime rib roast. In fact, you could use a rolled prime rib roast instead of the baron. Both cuts produce a very tasty tender roast.

Count on 1 pound (500 g) serving 2 people. Allow extra meat if using rolled prime rib.

Preheat oven to 300°F (150°C).

Place on rack in roasting pan. If oven space is a problem, stand the roast on end. Roast uncovered until meat thermometer reads 140°F (60°C) for rare meat, 160°F (75°C) for medium done, 170°F (90°C) for well done.

It is usually safest to roast to medium and then serve outside cuts to those who want their meat well or medium done, reserving inside slices for those who like it rare.

As you carve and serve meat, spoon on juices left in pan.

Western Baked Beans

Beef and beans go together like sunshine and picnics! And this version of baked beans is especially good with its mixture of beans in a sweet and sour sauce.

28 ounces	796 mL	baked beans (1 can)
28 ounces	796 mL	red kidney beans (1 can)
2 x 14 ounces	2 x 398 mL	lima beans, drained (2 cans)
19 ounces	540 mL	chick peas, drained (1 can)
¾ cup	175 mL	brown sugar
1 teaspoon	5 mL	dry mustard
1 teaspoon	5 mL	salt
½ teaspoon	2 mL	garlic powder
4 tablespoons	60 mL	ketchup
¾ cup	175 mL	vinegar

Preheat oven to 350°F (180°C).

In large pot or casserole dish, combine beans.

Mix sugar, seasonings, ketchup and vinegar and stir into beans.

Cover and bake for 30 minutes. Remove lid and bake uncovered for another 30 minutes or until hot and bubbly.

Serves 10.

Marinated Onions in Sour Cream

At a Beef and Bean Feast, the beef is often served on a bun. There's nothing better on top of that meat than Sour Cream Onions!

2	2	large onions, thinly sliced
½ cup	125 mL	vinegar
½ cup	125 mL	water
¾ cup	175 mL	sugar
1 cup	250 mL	sour cream
		salt and pepper to taste

Slice onions. Cover with vinegar, water and sugar to marinate for at least 6 hours.

Drain well. Mix with sour cream, salt and pepper.

Serves 10.

Marinated Tomato and Onion Salad

This is a snappy accompaniment for Beef and Beans, or for Hot Beef Sandwiches. It is particularly attractive if arranged in a shallow serving dish.

3	3	large onions, thinly sliced
6	6	medium tomatoes, thinly sliced
1 cup	250 mL	salad oil
⅔ cup	150 mL	vinegar
2 tablespoons	30 mL	sugar
1 teaspoon	5 mL	salt
1 teaspoon	5 mL	basil
		parsley and pepper to taste

Slice onions and tomatoes very thinly and place in bowl.

Mix remaining ingredients, pour over vegetables and let marinated for at least 4 hours.

Serves 10.

Air Buns

Dozens of round feather-light air buns are made for brandings and barbecues. They disappear as if into thin air.

½ cup	125 mL	warm water
1 teaspoon	5 mL	sugar
1 tablespoon	15 mL	yeast (1 pkg.)
3½ cups	875 mL	warm water
½ cup	125 mL	sugar
½ cup	125 mL	vegetable oil
1 tablespoon	15 mL	salt
2 teaspoons	10 mL	vanilla
8-10 cups	2-2.5 L	flour

Preheat oven to 400°F (200°C).

Pour the ½ cup (125 mL) warm water into large mixing bowl. Dissolve sugar, sprinkle the yeast on top and leave for 10 minutes.

Combine remaining water, sugar, vegetable oil, salt and vanilla and add to yeast mixture.

Beat in as much of flour mixture as possible; knead in remainder until dough no longer sticks to your hands or bowl. Knead for another 8 to 10 minutes.

Cover with tea towel and leave in warm place to rise for 1 hour.

Shape dough into round buns and place on greased cookie sheet – about 20 on an average cookie sheet.

Cover with tea towel and let rise again for approximately 1½ hours.

Bake for 12 to 15 minutes.

Yields 48 buns.

> *"So farewell to Alberta, farewell to the west,*
> *It's backwards I'll go to the girl I love best.*
> *I'll go back to the east and get me a wife*
> *And never eat cornbread the rest of my life."*
> *The Alberta Homesteader*

Saskatoon Pie

Saskatoons grow in every Canadian province but were most loved and used by prairie settlers. Even now families scout the gentle slopes and banks of streams in summer to pick enough berries for a taste of Saskatoon Pie. This recipe makes a thick and luscious pie.

		pastry for 2-crust 9" (23 cm) pie
4 cups	1 L	saskatoons
¼ cup	50 mL	water
2 tablespoons	30 mL	lemon juice
1 cup	250 mL	sugar
3 tablespoons	45 mL	flour*
¼ teaspoon	1 mL	salt
1 teaspoon	5 mL	grated lemon rind

Preheat oven to 400°F (200°C).

Prepare pastry recipe, page 165, and cover bottom of pie place.

Simmer saskatoons and water in covered saucepan for 5 minutes.

Mix in lemon juice, sugar, flour or tapioca, salt and lemon rind. Pour into uncooked pastry shell.

Top with another layer of pastry. Press edges with fork and make several slits in top for steam to escape.

Bake for 40 to 45 minutes or until lightly browned and fruit is tender. Serve with thick cream or Homemade Ice Cream, page 15.

*Note: In place of flour, you could use 2 tablespoons (30 mL) tapioca.

Deep Apple Pie

A "deep" apple pie differs from other pies in that there is no bottom crust and the filling is a bit thicker. Serve Canadian style with a piece of Cheddar cheese, or serve with Basic Butterscotch Sauce, Rum Sauce or Brandy Sauce.

		pastry to cover 9 x 13" (23 x 33 cm) baking dish
8 cups	2 L	sliced apples
1⅓ cups	325 mL	brown sugar
4 tablespoons	60 mL	flour
1½ teaspoons	7 mL	cinnamon
½ teaspoon	2 mL	nutmeg
4 tablespoons	60 mL	melted butter

Preheat oven to 400°F (200°C).

If using fresh apples core and peel. Slice into even pieces and place in greased 9 x 13" (23 x 33 cm) baking dish.

Combine sugar, flour, cinnamon and nutmeg and spread over apples so that they are evenly coated. Drizzle butter over top.

Roll pastry to rectangle larger than pan size. Place loosely over fruit, seal edge and cut vents.

Bake for 40 minutes for fresh applies, about 20 minutes longer for frozen applies.

Serves 10.

Note: You could use 2 packages frozen apples, 2 pounds (1 kg) each, in place of fresh apples. If using frozen, rinse under hot tap water to remove the ice crystals. Drain well.

Basic Butterscotch Sauce

This wonderful sauce for cake, puddings, ice cream, deep-dish apple pies and/or Christmas pudding can be changed with a simple change of flavoring. For instance, rum is good with Apple Pie, butterscotch with Ice Cream, brandy with Christmas Pudding.

¾ cup	175 mL	brown sugar
½ cup	125 mL	corn syrup
¼ cup	50 mL	butter
		dash salt
1 tablespoon	15 mL	cornstarch
1 cup	250 mL	water
1 teaspoon	5 mL	vanilla

In heavy saucepan, simmer sugar, corn syrup, butter and salt for about 4 minutes, stirring frequently. Mix cornstarch with about ½ of the water and stir in. Add remaining water and simmer for 2 to 3 minutes. Remove from head and add vanilla.

Rum Sauce:

Add 1 tablespoon (15 mL) rum to the Basic Butterscotch recipe.

Brandy Sauce:

Add 1 tablespoon (15 mL) brandy to the Basic Butterscotch recipe.

Rhubarb Crisp

Easy to prepare and serve, impossible to resist! Can be made ahead and reheated or served cold. Either way, your guests will want more.

8 cups	2 L	finely cut rhubarb
1⅓ cups	325 mL	sugar
1 teaspoon	5 mL	cinnamon
4 tablespoons	60 mL	water
⅔ cup	150 mL	flour
⅔ cups	150 mL	oatmeal
½ cup	125 mL	sugar
½ cup	125 mL	butter OR margarine

Preheat oven to 375°F (190°C).

Combine the 1⅓ cups (325 mL) sugar and cinnamon. Add to rhubarb and toss to coat evenly.

Place mixture in greased 9 x 13" (23 x 33 cm) baking pan. Sprinkle with water.

Combine flour, oatmeal and ½ cup (125 mL) sugar. Melt butter or margarine and mix with dry ingredients until crumbs form. Sprinkle over rhubarb.

Bake for 35 to 40 minutes if using fresh rhubarb, 50 to 60 minutes if using frozen.

Serve with thick cream or ice cream.

Serves 10.

British Columbia
Tastes of the land... and its history

Captain James Cook and crew were among the first known Europeans to land in what is now British Columbia. In 1778, they traded trinkets for sea otter furs with Indians in the Nootka Sound area, and they took time to brew spruce beer and salt down barrels of fish for the next sea voyage.

Alexander Mackenzie and his party for the Northwest Fur Trading Company were the first to cross the mountains into B.C. He wrote of meeting coastal Indians and feasting on "salmon roes pounded fine and beat up with water so as to have the appearance of cream", of "feasts of roasted salmon and berries – gooseberries, whortle berries and raspberries of fine quality".[1]

Others followed, building forts and trading posts all the way from Alaska to California. Fort Victoria was built on Vancouver Island as a seaport and soon after that, the Island was declared a Crown Colony. A governor was appointed and British gentry and servant settlers were encouraged to immigrate. The voyage was so long and dangerous that many never arrived but those who did brought silver, fine china, bonnets and crinolines. There in the midst of 30,000 Indians, they built English country homes, planted English gardens and introduced the gentlemen's life complete with balls, picnics and polite dinner conversation.

On the mainland, the fur trade was gearing down when news came that would change the area forever. Gold was discovered on the Fraser River.

Shiploads of men – and a few women – made their way to the gold fields carrying beans, bacon, flour, picks, shovels, gold pans, axes, cross bars and augers.

The Governor of Vancouver Island proclaimed that all gold mining territory belonged to the British Crown and that prospectors must obtain a mining license. Thus the mainland was declared the colony of British Columbia. Thousands of miners, with and without licenses, moved north along the Fraser River to Lillooet and thence to the Caribou. They picked their way over slippery trails, fallen logs, roots, rocks, gorges and precipices. Eventually, the famous Caribou Wagon Road was built, 18 feet wide so that wagon trains, ox trains, mule trains, coaches and stages could pass and meet on the way to and from Barkerville.

Roadhouses were built every 10 to 12 miles along the road to serve as hotels and supply depots. There travelers could buy a hot meal, have a drink from a bar, sleep on a hay mattress and stock up on flour, beans, bacon, potatoes, coffee, tea and hay for the next part of the trip.

At the gold fields, the diet was Caribou Turkey (bacon) and Caribou Strawberries (beans), sometimes supplemented by fish or wild game. Enterprising cowboys drove cattle from California and Oregon to feed the miners, receiving top prices for their beef, as you might guess!

After the mining operations slowed down, cowboys and roadhouse operators concentrated on ranching and established some of the big British Columbia cattle ranches. Work was hard and "grub" plain – plenty of hot biscuits, fried salt pork, beans or rice and always stewed prunes to "keep a fellow in good order".

The colonies of Vancouver Island and British Columbia united and joined the Dominion of Canada in 1871. The capital city of Victoria remained "a little bit of old England with tennis, cricket, polo, rugby, picnics, and afternoon tea", whereas Vancouver sprang to life as a bustling business center.

The food of British Columbia comes from both land and sea. Salmon is king but there's also fresh cod, red snapper, halibut, trout, perch, tuna, skate or sturgeon. Or, if you prefer shellfish, there're scallops, mussels, clams, oysters, shrimp, abalone and crab. Prime beef comes from the grazing lands of the Thompson, Chilcotin and Caribou. Fruits and vegetables are grown abundantly on farms and orchards in the interior of the province. Even roadsides yield berries – blackberries, blueberries, Oregon grapes, Saskatoons, strawberries and salmonberries.

It's an embarrassment of riches, that's what it is as far as food in British Columbia is concerned.

Celebrate the foods of British Columbia!

West Coast Feast

Salmon was life for the Indians of British Columbia. Fresh, smoked, dried – all forms were enjoyed.

The favorite was whole salmon split down the middle, fastened between split cedar shakes, suspended over the fire and slowly roasted to become lightly browned and gently smoked. Haida Indians slathered the fish during roasting with eluachon oil, the oil of another fish, but today's cooks use vegetable oil, perhaps a bit of lemon juice, salt and garlic.

Through the years, salmon became a favorite with all West Coast residents – whether cooked Haida-style over an open fire or barbecued backyard-style over a gas flame. There are five species of Pacific salmon to enjoy; Chinook, the largest and most highly prized as a game fish; Coho, red in color and very good for eating; Sockeye, deep red in color and particularly good for canning; Pink, delicately flavored, good for eating and less expensive; Chum, also known as Keta or Dog Salmon, the cheapest grade of salmon.

So, salmon must be the star of the West Coast feast. With it, we suggest Parsleyed Potatoes, preferably fresh from one of British Columbia's market gardens; asparagus which teams up so well with salmon; Cucumbers in Sour Cream which are another natural partner for salmon… and finally Peaches Flambé. An elegant dessert that uses the best of B.C. peaches.

MENU
● ● ● ●

Curried Cream of Broccoli Soup
Crusty French Bread
Haida Salmon
Parsleyed Potatoes
Fresh Asparagus
Cucumbers in Sour Cream
Peaches Flambé

Curried Cream of Broccoli Soup

This gently flavored soup makes an excellent beginning to many meals and serves as a luncheon soup as well. When entertaining, make soup a day ahead and refrigerate. Reheat to serve.

3 tablespoons	45 mL	butter
2	2	medium onions, chopped
1	1	garlic clove, minced
1 teaspoon	5 mL	curry powder
¼ teaspoon	1 mL	ground ginger
3 tablespoons	45 mL	flour
4 cups	1 L	chicken stock*
1½ pounds	750 g	broccoli, chopped
		salt and pepper to taste
1 cup	250 mL	cream, light OR whipping

In a large heavy-bottomed saucepan, melt butter, sauté onion and garlic until tender. Add curry powder and ginger and cook for 1 minute.

Add flour, cook and stir for 1 minute.

Add chicken stock, broccoli, salt and pepper to taste. Simmer for 35 minutes or until broccoli is very tender. Puree small amounts of soup in blender, food mill or food processor.

Return to saucepan. Stir in cream. Adjust seasonings. Heat through and serve.

Serves 8 to 10.

*Note: Chicken stock may be made by simmering necks and backs of chicken in water for 1½ hours, or use 4 to 6 chicken bouillon cubes dissolved in 4 cups (1 L) water.

Fresh Asparagus

Fresh tender asparagus is delicious with roasted salmon. Allow about 4 medium stalks per person.

Trim asparagus so that all stalks are the same length. Have a suitable sized pot or steamer ready so that asparagus can be steamed just before salmon is ready. A Pyrex coffee pot is good for this purpose – holds the stalks upright.

Steam in water for 7 to 10 minutes or just until tender. Drain.

Serve with a small bowl of mayonnaise for guests to spoon over asparagus as they wish.

Haida Salmon

This is an easy way to obtain the flavor of historic roasted Haida salmon. Prepare barbecue so that oiled grate is 4-5" (10-12 cm) from coals. Or make fire in fire pit and arrange grate about 12" (30 cm) above coals. Let barbecue or fire burn down to hot coals.

whole fresh salmon
coarse salt and freshly
ground pepper
powdered garlic
vegetable oil and lemon juice

Split salmon down back bone, right through as far as back skin, and lay flat. Thus the flesh is cut through but skin remains intact to that salmon is still in 1 piece.

Wipe flesh with paper towel.

Sprinkle with coarse salt, pepper and garlic powder.

Mix oil and lemon juice ½ and ½ and brush over flesh.

Place skin side down, directly on oiled grate. Roast fish 20 to 30 minutes, depending on thickness of fish and heat of coals, until white milky juices appear on top.

Brush occasionally with oil-lemon juice mixture

When done, remove fish to tray. Lift off the bone structure. Arrange attractively and garnish with lemon slices and parsley.

Parsleyed Potatoes

Potatoes were a staple of early Canadian tables – some men thought a meal incomplete unless it included "spuds" in some form or other. They would have liked this version of baked potatoes – simple but effective.

**small new potatoes, enough
for a crowd
butter, enough to rub outside
of potatoes
salt, pepper and chopped
parsley**

Scrub small new potatoes, allowing 1-2 potatoes per person, depending on size. If somewhat larger, cut in half. Simmer in pot of boiling salted water for about 10 minutes. Drain.

Rub potatoes with butter, sprinkle with salt, pepper and chopped parsley.

Wrap potatoes (2-3 in a package) in double layers of foil. Place packages on barbecue or edge of fire, about 4" (10 cm) from heat for approximately 15 minutes.

Preheat oven to 350°F (180°C) if you choose to oven bake.

Roast foil-wrapped potatoes in the oven for the entire cooking time (about an hour), in which case you wouldn't bother with the pre-cooking stage.

Cucumbers in Sour Cream

Canadians like cucumbers. A traveler to Québec in the 17th century wrote, "Cucumbers cut in slices and eaten with salt is a delicious dish. It is sometimes served plain; each diner secures one, peels it, cuts it into slices and eats it with salt, quite plain as one does a radish."[1]

2	2	large cucumbers
1 teaspoon	5 mL	salt
1 tablespoon	15 mL	vinegar
1 cup	250 mL	sour cream
1 teaspoon	5 mL	sugar
		freshly ground pepper and paprika
1 tablespoon	15 mL	chopped chives OR green onion

Slice cucumbers very thinly. Place in bowl and sprinkle with salt. Set aside for several hours. Drain well.

Combine vinegar, sour cream, sugar, pepper and paprika and mix well with drained cucumber. Place in serving bowl and sprinkle with chopped chives or green onions.

Peaches Flambé

This easily prepared elegant dessert can be brought to the table with great ceremony – in a chafing dish or other serving dish that will retain heat. Then light the flambé and wait for the compliments.

12	12	scoops of ice cream
4 cups	1 L	fresh peaches*
2 cups	500 mL	water
1½ cups	375 mL	brown sugar
1 teaspoon	5 mL	cinnamon
½ cup	125 mL	brandy

Place scoops of ice cream into serving bowl ahead of time and keep in the freezer until dessert time.

Peel and slice fresh peaches. Place in saucepan and add water, sugar and cinnamon. Simmer about 5 minutes.

Please into chafing dish or heat-proof dish and bring to table hot.

Heat brandy in small pan and bring to table also.

Pour brandy into peaches and as you do so, quickly hold lighted match to the brandy so that it can flame and add all sorts of drama to the occasion. Spoon hot mixture over ice cream.

*Note: For a winter dessert, heat canned sliced peaches in their own juice. Add 2 tablespoons (30 mL) brown sugar and complete with brandy as outlined above.

Notes

Nunavut
Tastes of the land... and its history

Until April 1, 1999, the vast territory in the Eastern Arctic of Canada was known simply as "The North" or "The Northwest Territories." It was big, it was cold, it was far away–that's about as much as many Canadians knew about the huge territories at the top of the map. But all that changed when the Canadian government created Nunavut as separate from the Northwest Territories, thus making three northern political entities–Nunavut, the Northwest Territories and the Yukon.

This newly named and constituted piece of Canada has an area roughly the size of British Columbia, Alberta and the Yukon combined. It's huge but there are only some 28 small isolated settlements scattered through the area with a population of approximately 27,000, most of whom are under the age of 25. Maybe that's where the push for more control of the government and resources of the area came from–the younger people who now have television and snowmobiles and e-mail. Fifty years ago, twenty years ago even, they would have been living semi-nomadic lives, depending on caribou and seals and other creatures of land and sea for their livelihood. Now, they're citizens of Nunavut and they have both the advantages and disadvantages of modern life.

Still, the land and sea underpin their lives, no matter the modern world. Many families return to hunting camps throughout the summer months, there to live as they would have years ago. That means meals of freshly caught meat and fish, sometimes eaten raw, sometimes cooked. One menu described in a recent magazine article began with the raw marrow out of a caribou bone, a real delicacy for the Inuit, followed by boiled goose, caribou and char. As the day progressed, more and more Inuit joined the party, bringing their own contributions of fresh food. Pretty soon they had a major party underway but it hadn't been planned as such. It just happened. That's the way of the north–to celebrate together when the time is right.

In 2003, the first ever Inuit Circumpolar Games were held. They featured various competitions demonstrating traditional survival skills, and one of the most popular was the "Good Woman" contest. To win that one, you had to be able to build a fire quickly, get water boiling for tea and turn out the fastest and tastiest bannock. It was no contest–the old women of the community won, hands down. After all, they had been travelling all their lives through some of the most desolate and difficult countryside anywhere and they had survived. Survival was a major accomplishment in that forbidding land.

Celebrate the foods of Nunavut!

Please Note:

The recipes in this section fudge a bit in that the meats and fish are cooked or roasted. The Whitefish Pate, for example, starts from cooked whitefish, but it brings with it a good story. Tell your guests that in years gone by they would have been eating the fish raw from the ocean. And, as for the Caribou Roast, they would have been eating all the entrails of the animal as well as the meat. Everything was used in the Inuit world. No waste, no want. They were ahead of their time.

Berries can only be picked in season in the north so the Berry Cake that is included would have been made in the summer only. Notice that there aren't a lot of berries in the cake. That's because the berries in the north were few and far between so that had to be used sparingly. However, that can be overcome nowadays with the help of modern supermarkets and year round berries.

Nunavut:
Food for Feasts and Gatherings

Feasts and gatherings in the north used to take place in the great outdoors, often as a picnic beside the sea. More often nowadays, however, they're held in a community hall where the women work their magic in the kitchen while the men and young folk wait impatiently at long tables. Sometimes, long sheets of cardboard are unrolled on the floor to be used as tables so that there's room for everyone. Generally there's soup to start everything off–soup made from seal meat, caribou meat or wild goose. Then there's frozen seal meat, whale meat and Arctic char, some of it to be eaten raw. There's also dried caribou meat and dried fish, both of which can be dipped into fermented seal fat, a traditional dish that tastes something like strong cheese. And with everything, there's good strong tea. Always tea.

If you'd like more ideas for the north, refer to the Northwest Territories section. There are recipes there for Arctic Char, Labrador Tea and Bannock, all of which apply to the Eastern Arctic regions of Nunavut as well.

MENU
● ● ● ●
Whitefish Paté
Assorted Crackers
Caribou Rib Roast or other Wild Game Roast
Cranberry Sauce... page 85
Mashed Potatoes
Berry Cake
Hot Labrador Tea... page 265

Whitefish Paté

An appetizer to toast the newest Canadian territory!

8 ounce	250 g	cooked whitefish
8 ounce	250 g	plain cream cheese
1 tablespoon	15 mL	onions, finely chopped
¾ teaspoon	4mL	curry powder
		mayonnaise

Flake the whitefish. Add cream cheese, onion, curry powder and enough mayonnaise to make paté easy to spread. Blend together and chill until serving.

Caribou Rib Roast

The summer diet of the caribou–lichens, grasses, plants and dwarf shrubs–results in a meat that is tender, tasty and very lean. If you can't get caribou, however, use other wild meats.

5 pounds	2.5 kg	caribou roast
2 tablespoons	30 mL	bacon fat
½ teaspoon	2 mL	salt
½ teaspoon	2 mL	pepper
4 tablespoons	60 mL	flour
3	3	onions
1½ cups	375 mL	beef bouillon
¼ cup	50 mL	red wine

Wipe roast with a damp cloth. Rub all the surfaces with bacon fat. Sprinkle with salt, pepper and 2 tablespoons (30 mL) flour. Place in roaster and add onions, beef bouillon and wine or vinegar. Cover and place in a 450° F or 230° C preheated oven for 30 minutes. Reduce oven to 350° F or 160° C and continue roasting for 2 hours or until tender. Add more liquid if necessary. Dissolve remaining 2 tablespoons (30 mL) flour in a little bit of water and slowly stir into the juices. Simmer for 10 minutes. Serve gravy with the meat.

You can substitute 2 tablespoons (30 mL) of red wine vinegar or balsamic vinegar for the red wine.

Berry Cake

¾ cup	175 mL	softened butter
1¼ cups	300 mL	sugar
1	1	egg
1¾ cups	425 mL	flour
1 tablespoon	15 mL	baking powder
1 teaspoon	5 mL	salt
1½ cups	375 mL	water
1 teaspoon	5 mL	vanilla
1 cup	250 mL	berries

Preheat oven to 350° F (180° C). Cream butter and sugar, add egg, add dry ingredients alternately with the water. Add vanilla. Fold in the berries. Fold into a greased cake pan and bake for 20-25 minutes.

Serve plain if you want to be authentic, or add icing or ice cream to the mix.

Northwest Territories
Tastes of the land... and its history

In the Northwest Territory you can eat the very latest in trendy foods. Or you might try partially digested moss and herbs from the stomach of a caribou or the rich butter-like marrow from a cracked caribou leg bone or a thin slice of muktuk from a freshly caught whale or boiled seal meat mixed with onions. Then too, you could look for the middle ground somewhere and enjoy Caribou Stew, Baked Arctic Char and Raisin Bannock.

The Territories, the largest land division in Canada, are sparsely populated with Inuit and Dene – both native names for "people". Together, they make up 58% of the population with the white population accounting for 42%. Generally, the Inuit live along the coastal rim and on the Arctic Islands whereas the Dene or Northern Indians live in the inland forested area. Most of the white population lives in the larger communities such as Yellowknife, capital of the Territories, or Hay River or Fort Smith.

The Arctic region looks harsh and cruel but it's not the frozen waste that it first appears to be. Seas teem with fish and once supported a prosperous whaling industry. Forests are home to rich fur-bearing animals and to this day support many trappers and traders. The hills and rocks yield minerals – zinc, lead, gold, silver and tungsten, and recently the frozen tundra and ice have given up rich stores of oil and gas.

Both the Inuit and Dene lifestyles are in transition. Up to 30 years ago, most lived in snow houses or skin tents and moved camp to find food as the seasons changed. Their possessions were few: skins for warmth, a few cooking pots and implements, a stone lamp for heating and light.

Meat was the most important item in the Inuit diet as shown by the fact that the word for meat (nirkit) is also the word for food. Food thus was caribou, seal, arctic hare, musk-ox, polar bear, walrus, Beluga whale, fish and ptarmigan with the occasional berries, herbs, willow buds, roots and seaweed thrown in when available. One visitor wrote, "During our stay we feasted on caribou tongues and a range of other foods. Eating all parts of an animal – back fat, raw bone marrow, liver and intestines – as well as seagull eggs, fish heads and other marvels gave us a balanced diet and provided us with a world of flavors."[1]

However, that visitor would just as likely get a TV dinner if he were to visit today.

Life for the Dene has also changed. Their ancestors have lived in the Mackenzie Basin for thousands of years using snowshoes, toboggans, snares, bows and arrows, fish nets, spears and guns to obtain whatever sparse living they were able to accomplish. The main burden for obtaining food fell on the male hunters but everyone had to do their part, with women and children snaring hares when other food was scarce.

Caribou and fish were the most important sources of food. Sheep, goats, musk-ox, wood buffalo, moose, elk, deer, bear, beaver, porcupine, muskrat, marmot and hares were also hunted. Summer provided some welcome variety – migratory waterfowl, ptarmigan, eggs, shellfish, roots, berries, lichen, bulbs and sweep sap from birch trees. Fish were split open and smoked in summer, frozen during the winter. Pemmican was prepared from whatever meat was on hand.

The modern world has caught up with most northerners, a fact that leads to some interesting combinations of old and new. A journalist wrote that, "A hunter going up the Eastmain River may use his skin drum in a ceremony to find caribou and his transistor radio to listen for news. A hostess at Eskimo Point will cut potatoes with her ulu but slice the caribou roast with an electric carving knife."

All of which means that food is not predictable in the north. Expect surprises!

Celebrate the foods
of the Northwest Territories!

Snow Villages

Early white visitors were fascinated by the snow villages of the Inuit. In many, a number of family dwellings were grouped around a central dancing house.

Many still alive today were born in snow houses or skin tents, and remember hunting for caribou, musk oxen, polar bears, walrus, seals and Beluga whales.

Mug-Up and Northern Dinner

After traveling many miles to visit friends, Canadians of the Northwest Territories are not about to eat and run. No way. First they'll stop for a Mug-Up, a good visit over tea and bannock. Then they'll stay for supper and continue their fellowship... which is why we have a two-part menu in this section; one for tea and one for supper.

Northern hospitality decrees that one's door must be open to all who pass, and food must be offered to everyone. It's no wonder that northern homemakers learned to always have tea on hand plus the makings for bannock. Bannock is a many splendored thing – a quick bread that is sometimes fried, sometimes baked. In the early days, it varied enormously according to the ingredients available but it's been standardized in the last few years so that we can all try our hand at it.

For a taste of the arctic at supper time, we have featured Arctic Char on our menu. With the accompanying Lemon Butter Sauce, it's about as good as you're going to get! To go along with it, we've suggested Wild Rice, and for dessert – a Rhubarb Fool, a recipe that has nothing to do with being a fool but everything to do with delicious. Rhubarb grows wild in some parts of the Northwest Territories but modern cooks can find it, growing tame, right in their frozen food cases in supermarkets.

MENU

● ● ● ●

Bannock and Cranberry Jam
Hot Labrador Tea
Grilled Arctic Char with Lemon-Butter Sauce
Wild Rice... page 218
Dilled Green Beans... page 77
Rhubarb Fool
Cranberry Loaf

Bannock

Bannock is the bread of Canada's earliest settlers, the fur traders and buffalo hunters. When flour became available to native Indians, they also began making bannock until eventually it became thought of as their traditional food. This recipe includes instructions for frying or baking bannock. Try it someday – as a change from other, more standard quick breads.

3 cups	750 mL	flour
3 tablespoons	45 mL	baking powder
1 teaspoon	5 mL	salt
2 tablespoons	30 mL	melted lard
1½ cups	375 mL	water

Preheat oven to 400°F (200°C).

Combine dry ingredients. Make a depression and pour in melted lard and water. Mix into a soft dough and gently knead a few times.

To fry: Shape the dough into a flat piece. Cut into rectangles. Heat about ½" (1.5 cm) of hot fat in frying pan. Drop a few pieces of dough at a time into the hot fat. When browned on 1 side, turn over and cook other side. Drain on paper towels.

To bake: Shape dough into 1 single flat round cake or 12 small flat round cakes. Place on greased baking sheet and bake for about 20 minutes or until top is brown.

Serve with homemade Cranberry Jam (recipe on following page) or Strawberry Jam.

Cranberry Jam

3 cups	750 mL	cranberries
2 cups	500 mL	sugar
1 cup	250 mL	water
1 teaspoon	5 mL	cinnamon

Simmer ingredients in saucepan until mixture is thick and mushy. Chill and serve with quick breads or toast.

Labrador Tea

A good woman of the Far North had to make do with whatever she had on hand – which is why she learned to make a good cup of tea with Labrador tea leaves. The leaves come from a common shrub that grows in muskegs, bogs and wet forests of the north. It is still used by the Indians and Inuit in the north, although they also purchase tea bags – just like the rest of us!

If ever you meet a Labrador tea plant, collect some leaves and try your hand at tea making. A handful of leaves should be enough, steeped in 4 cups (1 L) boiling water. The result will be a yellowish green tea with a sweet flower-like fragrance.

Arctic Char

Arctic Char is a delicacy from the cold water of the Arctic in the most northern part of Canada. It resembles both salmon and trout in flavor, with a color ranging from white to salmon pink.

1	1	piece Arctic Char
		cheesecloth for wrapping the fish
		boiling water to cover
1 cup	250 mL	vinegar OR lemon juice

Preheat oven to 450°F (230°C).

Wrap fish in cheesecloth and tie ends. Place in roasting or broiling pan – whatever size will work – and almost cover with boiling water.

Add the vinegar or lemon juice. Cover pan with foil.

Poach for about 12 minutes per inch (2.5 cm) thickness. Serve with Lemon-Butter Sauce (below).

Lemon Butter Sauce

¼ cup	50 mL	butter
1 tablespoon	15 mL	lemon juice
¼ teaspoon	1 mL	grated lemon rind

Have butter at room temperature.

In small bowl, combine all ingredients and stir until well blended.

Sauce should be at room temperature when served over the fish.

Rhubarb Fool

"Fools" are part of Canada's food history; essentially, they're stewed fruit with added cream. This particular version of Rhubarb Fool was served in the dining room of the Northwest Territories Pavilion at EXPO'86, much to the delight of the many visitors who rediscovered this old favorite.

6 cups	1.5 L	diced rhubarb
1 cup	250 mL	water
¾ cup	175 mL	sugar
2 cups	500 mL	whipping cream

Simmer rhubarb with water until thick, soft and mushy. Add sugar. Chill.

Whip cream until thick. Fold into stewed rhubarb. Chill again.

Serve in tall parfait or sherbet glasses.

Serves 8.

Cranberry Loaf

Cranberries are very Canadian. They grow all over the country and were therefore used by our very first citizens – the Indians. Later settlers also learned to appreciate and use them in many different ways. Try this moist, tasty loaf – very nice for afternoon tea or coffee.

1 cup	250 mL	fresh OR frozen cranberries
⅓ cup	75 mL	sugar
⅓ cup	75 mL	sugar
2 cups	500 mL	flour
1 tablespoon	15 mL	baking powder
½ teaspoon	2 mL	salt
1 teaspoon	5 mL	cinnamon
1	1	egg, slightly beaten
1 cup	250 mL	milk
⅓ cup	75 mL	vegetable oil
¼ cup	50 mL	chopped walnuts

Preheat oven to 350°F (180°C).

Coarsely chop cranberries. Combine them with the first ⅓ cup (75 mL) sugar. Set aside.

Combine the remaining ⅓ cup (75 mL) sugar with flour, baking powder, salt and cinnamon.

In small bowl, combine egg, milk and vegetable oil and add to dry ingredients. Stir just until blended. Stir in walnuts.

Place in greased 8-cup (2 L) loaf pan.

Bake for 60 minutes or until loaf is light golden in color and tests clean with a toothpick.

Yukon
Tastes of the land... and its history

August 17, 1896, marked the beginning of the world's biggest gold rush. That was the day that George and Kate Carmack, Skookum Jim and Tagish Charley discovered gold on a tributary of the Klondike River.

Within two years, hordes of people from all over the world struggled over the many tortuous trails leading to Dawson City, packing their goods on the backs of animals or on their own backs. Many went quite unprepared for the life that awaited them. As one of the prospectors explained in his diary, "Food was the great problem of life in the district. Cold does not cause much worry, for men can wrap themselves warmly enough to guard against loss of life from exposure, but few things grow in the northern clime and there is a lack of animal food which can be scarified to support the life of man. Hence enormous prices are charged for provisions."[1]

Scurvy and starvation were the scourges of the first winter. There was such a shortage of food that the North West Mounted Police enforced a regulation at the border that no one could enter the Yukon Territory of Canada without a year's supply of food – roughly estimated to be 1,150 pounds. That, together with tools, equipment, tents and warm clothes, added up to as much as a ton of goods.[2]

The "stampeders" for gold staked their claims, panned for gold, set up tents and sluice boxes, built rough cabins, dance halls, saloons and gambling joints. Women arrived to work in the dance halls and saloons or to make their own fortunes in more mundane ways – as seamstresses or bakers or nurses.

The wife of one of the early commissioners of the territory had her own story to tell about living conditions in the north! Although she was grateful for the cold storage facilities by then available in Dawson City, she nevertheless yearned for some really fresh eggs. To this end, she went to Vancouver for six-dozen hens and once they were established, enjoyed each and every egg that she ate. Then she found out that the chickens had not prospered in the northern climate; all along her husband had been buying crates of cold storage eggs which she believed her gardener was delivering fresh from the hen house."[34]

By 1898, it was estimated that up to 40,000 people lived in the Yukon and that Dawson City was the largest city west of Winnipeg. Fortunately, the Mounted Police were established before the biggest rush of people and with help from the

Yukon Field Force kept law and order. The gold rush activities and boundary disputes with the United States caused the Canadian government to pass the Yukon Territories act in 1898, establishing the Yukon as a territory separate from the Northwest Territories. Both remain as "territories", not provinces, and are administered directly from Ottawa, the capital city of Canada.

Yellowknife became the capital city of the Yukon Territory and gradually, as the gold activity slowed, replaced Dawson City as the biggest city.

The rush for gold was over by the turn of the century but mining and minerals have remained the backbone of the economy: gold, silver, lead, zinc, copper, asbestos and coal. The white population accounts for about 75% of Yukon's population; Indians make up the remaining 25%. Like native people everywhere, the Indians of the Yukon are caught in a difficult transition between their old ways and the ways of the brave new world. Some still hunt and fish when possible, others depend upon government support.

Yukoner's fill their freezers with moose, other game and fish. Otherwise, the food of the Yukon is pretty much the same as food anywhere in Canada now, thanks to airplanes and ships that can make deliveries year round. However, Yukoners still take great pride in their gold rush beginnings and work them into menus, tourist attractions, and special celebrations. For instance, the Discovery Day celebrations in Dawson City every year feature sourdough in every way possible... and that's good news for those of us who have grown to appreciate that slightly sour, anything-but-boring taste!

Celebrate the foods of the Yukon!

Sourdough Rendezvous
under the Midnight Sun

Prospectors and miners who opened up the North used so much sourdough that the word alone conjures up visions of gold miners toiling up the Chilkoot, panning for gold. In fact, some gold miners got more sourdough than gold. In honor of the old standby, many Yukon centers hold an annual Sourdough Celebration – Sourdough Rendezvous in Whitehorse, Discovery Days in Dawson, just to name two. At these affairs, sourdough is used in everything possible – biscuits, pancakes, breads. Some old-timers predict that sourdough ice cream will be next!

In the early days, food supplies came in once or twice a year by ship and then had to be transferred to some other means of transportation for an even longer trip. As yeast had a short life, it was apt to deteriorate entirely before reaching its destination. Baking powder and baking soda weren't the answer either since an excess of either can cause stomach problems. So sourdough starter became a standby. It's a leavening agent and flavoring agent for bread products produced by the fermentation of flour and water; flour, water and sugar; flour, water, yeast and sugar. With care, it can be kept going indefinitely. When a portion is removed and equal amount of flour and water must be added back to the mixture for the microorganisms to work on. Otherwise, it will overact and spoil.

Our Sourdough rendezvous would be a perfect brunch combination. We've started out with the instructions for Sourdough Pancakes to be served with Mock Maple Syrup. If that isn't enough, and for the hearty appetites of the North, it wouldn't be enough, then serve Glazed Back Bacon and a pot full of traditional Baked Beans as well. Now, there's a breakfast/brunch/lunch to prepare you for the day!

MENU

Sourdough Pancakes
Mock Maple Syrup
Glazed Back Bacon
Traditional Baked Beans

Sourdough Pancakes

Genuine Sourdough Pancakes bring the zest of the Yukon into your kitchen. Remember there are 2 stages in preparation. First, make your starter several days ahead of time; then keep it forever, see page 265. Next, prepare the batter, using the starter, the night before your pancake feast.

The Starter:

1 tablespoon	15 mL	dry yeast
1 cup	250 mL	warm water
1½ tablespoons	25 mL	brown sugar
1 teaspoon	5 mL	salt
2 cups	500 mL	flour
1½ cups	375 mL	water

In bowl (not metal) dissolve yeast in warm water until bubbly. Stir in sugar, salt, flour and water.

Cover with plastic wrap or a cloth and let stand at room temperature for 2 to 3 days. Stir 2 to 3 times a day.

If room is very warm, you can slow fermentation by placing starter in refrigerator for a few hours. When starter is ready, it will give off a delicious, sour, yeasty odor.

(Continued on next page.)

(Continued)

The Pancakes:

1 cup	250 mL	sourdough starter
2½ cups	625 mL	flour
1½ teaspoons	7 mL	brown sugar
1 teaspoon	5 mL	salt
3 cups	750 mL	water
1	1	egg, beaten
1 teaspoon	5 mL	baking soda

Mix sourdough starter, flour, sugar, salt and water in large bowl (not metal). Allow to stand overnight, covered, at room temperature.

In the morning, beat in egg and baking soda. Spoon or ladle onto lightly buttered griddle. Bake until bubbles form on the top and batter is slightly set. Turn over and bake other side until lightly browned.

Mock Maple Syrup

If you don't have a maple syrup tree in the back yard, or a jar of Maple Syrup in your cupboard, this Mock Maple Syrup will do until the real thing comes along! It was widely used in pioneer homes.

2 cups	500 mL	brown sugar
1 cup	250mL	water
½ teaspoon	2 mL	maple flavoring

Bring brown sugar and water to a boil and simmer for about 5 minutes. Add flavoring. Store in container in refrigerator and serve hot or cold.

Glazed Back Bacon

A glazed roast of Back Bacon or Pea Meal Bacon is a Canadian specialty that is delicious for breakfast, brunch, dinner or sandwiches. One pound (500 g) should serve 4 to 5 people, depending on the time of day and the appetites in question!

3 pounds	1.5 kg	back bacon
1½ cups	375 mL	apple juice
¼ cup	50 mL	brown sugar
1 teaspoon	5 mL	dry mustard
10-12	10-12	whole cloves

Preheat oven to 400°F (200°C).

Place bacon in saucepan just big enough to hold it. Pour apple juice over top. Liquid should completely cover meat, so add water if necessary. Cover and simmer for 30 minutes per pound, 60 minutes, per kg.

Remove meat from liquid. Reserve liquid.

Mix brown sugar and mustard and pat over top of bacon. Poke whole cloves over top.

Bake for 20 minutes or until browned. Occasionally, spoon some apple juice liquid over top.

Serve hot or cold. Carve into thin slices.

Roast Moose

Perhaps moose meat is the most coveted and sought after of all the big game meats. Moose range through Great Slave Lake, Great Bear Lake and Mackenzie Valley from the 60th parallel almost to the Arctic Ocean as well as part of the Keewatin District of the Northwest Territories and Newfoundland. Historic writing also recalls the plentiful use of moose meat in the Atlantic Provinces.

Traditional Baked Beans

*All over Canada, people claim baked beans as their own. In the
Maritimes, a crock of beans was the Saturday night supper with
leftovers served up for Sunday breakfast. Hungry loggers in Québec
ate beans and salt pork twice a day – whether they wanted to or not!
Prospectors claim that "beans opened up Ontario's mines". Because
they kept well over cold winters, they were a standby for prairie cooks.
Beans traveled in the chuckwagons with the cattle herds; they went
over the Chilkoot to the gold fields and up north to the trappers'
cabins.*

2 pounds	1 kg	white beans*
		water to cover
1 teaspoon	5 mL	baking soda
1 pound	500 g	salt pork*
1½ tablespoons	25 mL	red wine vinegar
2 teaspoons	10 mL	dry mustard
1½ teaspoons	7 mL	salt
		pinch chili powder
		pinch black pepper
½ cup	125 mL	molasses
½ cup	125 mL	maple syrup
2 cups	500 mL	water (approximately)

Pour water over beans until water level is 2" (5 cm) higher than
beans and allow to soak overnight. In the morning, drain water off,
put beans into large saucepan, add baking soda and cover again with
water. (The baking soda is to alleviate the gas problem in beans.)
Simmer until beans are tender, 30 to 60 minutes, depending on the
kind of bean used. Drain and rinse with cold water.

Preheat oven to 300°F (150°C).

(Continued on next page.)

(Continued)

Place beans into a bean pot or large casserole dish. Cut salt pork into chunks and add. If using pork hocks, tuck them into the bean pot whole. Mix remaining ingredients, except water, and stir into beans. Add water to cover. Bake for 4 to 5 hours or bake overnight at 200°F (100°C). Add more water if necessary.

Serves 8 to 10.

*Notes: White beans include navy beans, pea beans or Great Northern beans. Instead of salt pork, you could use 2 pork hocks.

Note: If you don't have time to soak beans overnight, use the quick soak method. Combine 3 cups (750 mL) water for every cup (250 mL) of beans, bring water and beans to a boil for 2 minutes, then remove from heat and let stand for 1 hour. Then drain and add other ingredients as above.

Footnotes

Nova Scotia

1. Marie Nightingale, "Out of Old Nova Scotia Kitchens", H.H. Marshall Limited, 1970, p. 8
2. Helen Crighton, "Folklore of Lunenburg County, Nova Scotia". National Museum of Canada, Bulletin No. 117, Anthropological Series No. 25, King's Printer, Ottawa, 1950, p. 68
3. Helen Wilson, "When Mama Cooked Solomon Grundy", Maclean's Magazine, Nov. 16, 1964, p. 27.

Prince Edward Island

1. Stuart Trueman, "Don't Let Them Smell the Lobsters Cooking", McClelland and Stewart Limited, Toronto, 1982.
2. Margaret Galloway, "I Lived in Paradise" (Winnipeg Bulman Brothers Limited, (n.d.) p. 186.

Québec

1. Raymond Douville and Jacques Casanova, "Daily Life in Early Canada". Translated by Carola Congreves. London, Allen and Unwin Ltd. 1968.
2. Ibid.
3. Ibid.

Ontario

1. Walter Stewart, "True Blue, The Loyalist Legend", Collins Publishers, Toronto, 11985, p. 176.
2. Anna Leveridge in Bev Hykel, "Feeding the Nineteenth Century Family", Ontario Museum Association Quarterly, Summer 1979, Vol 8, No. 3, p. 9.
3. Diary of Bertha Hamden, Archives of Ontario, Toronto.

Manitoba

1. Charles Mair (a letter written November 27, 1868 and published several weeks later in the Toronto Globe) in W. J. Healy, "Women of the Red River", Women's Canadian Club, Winnipeg, 1923, p. 129.

Footnotes

Alberta

1. Paul Kane's Frontier: including Wanderings of an Artist among the Indians of North America, Ed. By J. Russell Harper. Published for the Amon Carter Museum of Western Art and the National Gallery of Canada by the University of Texas Press, 1971, pp. 138-139.

British Columbia

1. Raymond Douville and Jacques Casanova, Daily Life in Early Canada. Translated by Carola Congreves. London, Allen and Unwin, 1968, p. 55.

Northwest Territories

1. Yva Momatiuk and John Eastcott, "Still Eskimo, Still Free", National Geographic, Nov. 1977, p. 642. Keith J. Crowe, A History of the Original Peoples of Northern Canada, Arctic Institute of North America. Queen's University Press, Montreal and London, 1974, p. 210.

Yukon

1. A.C. Harris, "Alaska and the Klondike Gold Fields", originally published 1867, facsimile published by Coles Publishing Co. Toronto, 1972, p. 35.
2. Pierre Berton, "Klondike", McClelland and Stewart Limited, Toronto, 1983, p. 154.
3. J.B. McDougall, "The Yukon Trail", McDougall and Secord Guide to the Gold Fields, Edmonton, 1897.
4. Margaret Archibald, "Grubstake to Grocery Store: Supplying the Klondike", 1897-1907. Prepared by National Parks and Sites Branch and published under the authority of the Minister of the Environment, Ottawa, p. 80.

Index

Index

Index

Index

Index

Index

Index

Index

Index